An Easily Bewildered Child

ALSO BY ROY FISHER

POETRY
City (Migrant Press), 1961
Interiors: Ten Interiors with Various Figures (Tarasque Press), 1966
The Ship's Orchestra (Fulcrum Press), 1966
The Memorial Fountain (Northern House), 1966
Collected Poems 1968 (Fulcrum Press), 1968
Matrix (Fulcrum Press), 1971
The Cut Pages (Fulcrum Press), 1971
The Thing About Joe Sullivan (Carcanet Press), 1978
Poems 1955–1980 (Oxford University Press), 1980
The Cut Pages (Oasis Books & Shearsman Books), 1986
A Furnace (Oxford University Press), 1986
Poems 1955–1987 (Oxford University Press), 1988
Birmingham River (Oxford University Press), 1994
The Dow Low Drop — New and Selected Poems (Bloodaxe Books), 1996
The Long and the Short of It — Poems 1955–2005 (Bloodaxe Books), 2005
Standard Midland (Bloodaxe Books), 2010
Selected Poems (Flood Editions), 2011

ESSAYS / INTERVIEWS / PROSE
Roy Fisher: *Nineteen Poems and an Interview* (Grosseteste Press), 1975
Robert Sheppard & Peter Robinson (eds.): *News for the Ear: a homage to Roy Fisher*
        (Stride Publications), 2000
Peter Robinson & John Kerrigan (eds.): *The Thing About Roy Fisher: Critical
        Essays on the Poetry of Roy Fisher* (Liverpool University Press), 2000
Peter Robinson (ed.): *An Unofficial Roy Fisher* (Shearsman Books), 2010
Tony Frazer (ed.): *Interviews Through Time* (Shearsman Books), 2013

An Easily Bewildered Child

Occasional Prose 1963-2013

Roy Fisher

EDITED BY PETER ROBINSON

Shearsman Books

This second, revised edition published in the United Kingdom in 2014 by
Shearsman Books
50 Westons Hill Drive
Emersons Green
BRISTOL BS16 7DF

Shearsman Books Ltd Registered Office
30–31 St. James Place, Mangotsfield, Bristol BS16 9JB
(this address not for correspondence)

www.shearsman.com

ISBN 978-1-84861-300-3

Copyright © Roy Fisher, 1963-2014.
Introduction and Note on the Text copyright © Peter Robinson, 2014.
All rights reserved.

ACKNOWLEDGEMENTS
We are grateful to Bloodaxe Books for permission to reprint Roy Fisher's poems
'One World', 'Magritte Imitated Himself', 'The Memorial Fountain', 'After Working', and 'The Home Pianist's Companion' from the author's *The Long and the Short of It: Poems 1955-2005* (Bloodaxe Books, Tarset, 2005).

*Details of the original publication of the author's writings included in this volume
may be found in the Checklist by Derek Slade, commencing on p.192.*

CONTENTS

Author Note	8
Introduction	9
Note on the Text	14

I. ANTEBIOGRAPHY

Meanwhile	17
Antebiography	20
Brum Born	48
Talks for Words	51
The Morden Tower	62
My Trip to Brighton	63
Six Towns	65
Memoir of Richard Caddel	67
At the Funeral of Stuart Mills	69
License My Roving Hands	70

II. ROY FISHER ON ROY FISHER

Poet on Writing	99
Note on *The Cut Pages*	103
Roy Fisher writes…	104
Handsworth Compulsions	106
Preface to *A Furnace*	109
Birmingham's What I Think With: Programme Note	111
Reply to Paul Lester	112
Inside *A Various Art*	119
Roy Fisher on Roy Fisher	133

III. ON POETS AND OTHERS

Death by Adjectives	139
David Prentice	143
The Green Fuse	145
Mary Fitton's Foreshores	150

On John Cowper Powys' Letters	151
Thomas Campion	158
On a Study of Dada	159
On Ezra Pound	163
Debt to Mr Bunting	165
At a Tangent	170
On a Study of Robert Creeley	172
On Kenneth Rexroth's *An Autobiographical Novel*	174
Gael Turnbull	177
Foreword to *Spleen* (Nicholas Moore/Baudelaire)	178
Introduction to Jeff Nuttall's *Selected Poems*	181
Concerning Joseph Brodsky	182
Coat Hanger	188
A Checklist of Roy Fisher's Occasional Prose by Derek Slade	192

i.m. Ann Atkinson

Author Note

When a poem looks complete and I can see what it has turned out to be, I don't expect to find surprises if I revisit. It either has a life of its own or none. With a prose piece that has no claim to be art the case is different: so an essay, an obituary, a reminiscence, a review or even, in another life, a syllabus or a notice-board announcement may look ordinary but is for me stranger than a poem and invites looking at again and again. It's not entirely mine in its origin and I quite often play a game that involves sneaking up on the published text, stepping outside myself and judging it as though somebody else had written it. Most of the pieces in this book have had this treatment: all of them owe their origins to commissions, suggestions or various forms of pressure from friends.

Roy Fisher
November 2013

INTRODUCTION

Peter Robinson

An Easily Bewildered Child, Roy Fisher's choice of title for this collection of his occasional prose, is the first clause in the opening sentence of 'Meanwhile' (2012). No sooner has he recalled this state of mind than he evokes another world "sewn like a lining into the customary" one. Its "shadowy synesthesia" is felt to have "tones and imperatives of its own" and comes as the explanation, a private one never discussed by the child with anybody else, for Fisher's youthful attraction first to painting, then jazz music, and eventually poetry, his third art and the one that still hasn't "run out of road"—his poem 'Signs and Signals' was written for Carol Ann Duffy's centenary anthology *1914: Poetry Remembers* by a poet in his ninth decade. Fisher's intuited and yet barely articulated association between his states of mind as a child and later, and his unusually distinctive aesthetic inquiry into the world in which he found himself, is one of the recurring fascinations of the writings gathered here.

In his 'Antebiography' (1989) he similarly gives an account of the three-year period immediately after the Second World War in which the boy described as the Daft Kid at school believed himself, with no evidence, to be terminally ill. Again, he describes this as a renegotiation of his contract with the world, a renegotiation that it is implied is analogous to the relation an artist will need to develop with what for such an artist is also material with, as Fisher puts it, "tones and imperatives of its own". These orders of experience are offered as something to which the artist in him had to respond. Yet they are suspected of being characteristics that, for others, were not even there, were not "sewn like a lining into the customary world" at all.

Returning to Birmingham in the later 1950s, after a period as a teacher in Devon, Fisher's relationship to his birthplace was reordered, it appears, by his life as a semi-professional jazz pianist, playing in a great variety of venues and returning home in the small hours, living with a night person's relationship to the diurnal round. Fisher reports this period of his life as the circumstance behind the composition of the poetry and prose that would eventually be collaged into *City* (1961), his signature early work. Once again, though, and most evidently in *The Ship's Orchestra* (1965), in Fisher's work there is never a straightforward mimetic relation between sensory experience and its aesthetic ordering in poetry and prose. Among the fascinations of his occasional writings are the accounts he gives of his tastes, life events, and artistic allegiances, accounts that show how even the most distinctive of sensibilities finds self-understanding in relation to the experiences, artistic or not, of others.

This helps to indicate how it could be possible for readers who may well be among those others for whom no such "shadowy synesthesia" has been present from childhood to respond to his poetry and prose to the extent that his developing works have remained in print with a number of different publishers over more than fifty years. Again, these writings help us to see how Fisher's sensibility, easily bewildering when he was young and leaving traces on his mental life to this day, has associated itself with others' painting, music and poetry, with a loose grouping of poets responding to developments in American poetry that began to emerge in the late 1940s, became a rumour in Britain during the 1950s and found print with mainly small publishers in the 1960s, coextensive with the early publications of these same British poets.

Though Fisher decided not subsequently to reprint with its poem the preface included in the first edition of *A Furnace*, published by Oxford University Press in 1986, he did think it deserved preservation in such a collection of occasional prose as the present volume. The following note was also written to explain this publishing decision:

> When the original publication of the book-length poem *A Furnace* was in preparation the publisher asked me to provide an introduction that might make the book more 'accessible' to readers who needed that sort of thing. I complied after a fashion but was unwilling to write my own advertising copy and wanted the poem to be self-sufficient, which it has been allowed to be in all subsequent re-printings.

Self-sufficiency has thus now been extended both to the poem and to its introductory prose piece, and this, I think, gives a clue both to the nature and the justification for this collection of Fisher's occasional prose writings. Though dependent on their author's reputation and character as the writer of those self-sufficient works, these commissioned pieces, as Fisher's 'Author Note' explains, have another kind of self-sufficiency, one that appears to float free of their writer's imaginative life.

Unwilling to produce his own advertising copy, one might think of Fisher as the Bartleby of contemporary British poetry, and certainly this volume is marked by a number of tacit refusals and reluctances—refusals and reluctances, that is, to do the predictable or expected thing. Asked to compose an autobiographical sketch for an American reference work, Fisher chose to compose an account largely focused on his parents and grandparents, allowing the future poet into it only in so far as he was himself, as a boy, part of their subject matter and environment. Yet the resulting 'Antebiography' is one of his most sustained, sustaining, and enlightening pieces of occasional writing. It also serves as a first-class introduction to the sensibility and its cultural origins that came to write the imaginative poetry and prose for which he is most well known. In this, and characteristically, Fisher fulfilled the assignment by appearing not to do so.

Similarly, though no jacket-copy writer for himself, when asked by *The Rialto*, Fisher was not averse to writing the self-review 'Roy Fisher on Roy Fisher' (1996), in which he calls *A Furnace* "for all its unconscious or unashamed solipsism, one of the most ambitious recent English poems I've read." It is characteristically subtle of Fisher to qualify his poem's solipsism as both "unconscious" and "unashamed", for it would be impossible for him to be unashamed about it if it were unconscious and vice versa. Yet this self-review again gives him the opportunity simultaneously to know what he's talking about and speculate about it as if he didn't:

> With no gift for the anecdotal discursive, self-contained, teachable A4 poem, he's happiest at the extremes of duration: the three-or-four-line fragment or the forty-page long haul, and this takes us to the heart of what he's about. I think he's a Romantic, gutted and kippered by two centuries' hard knocks. The willingness to regard his sketch-books as exhibitable ('Diversions', 'It Follows That') and to go on shamanic mental trips though humdrum-looking material are the indicators. Either way, the technique is one of epiphanic revelation.

Thus, a further interest in reading Fisher's work is to understand how such a self-conception could issue in work which communicates to others, and gives no impression that the world which it evokes and explores is not the one shared with him. Illustrations of this are everywhere to see in 'Antebiography', for instance, where the young Fisher's emotional states, however unusual and remote, are conveyed in terms that make them perfectly intelligible and related to the circumstances of war or of a developing set of artistic stances towards the world. It also shows in the many and various accounts of others' behaviours, actions and works both in the memoirs and prompted critical forays gathered here.

One reason for taking up his characterization of *A Furnace* as manifesting "unconscious or unashamed solipsism" in the self-review is not only to make the point that to call yourself a solipsist is to be aware enough of your self among others in the world not to be one, but also to try and get a bearing on the relationship between his acute perception of and reflections on other people in his work, and the insistence, in his poem 'The Lesson in Composition' that, because art "stunts itself / to talk about the rest in the rest's own terms", he must "for a while ... seem to be away" from a "worldliness that sticks to me" so as to find in his material the art that can be made out of it. This is a further conundrum Fisher has explored, one which helps explain how his poetry can have a sustained political and ethical character, while overtly eschewing—as in 'It is Writing' where he will "mistrust the poem in its hour of success, / a thing capable of being / tempted by ethics into the wonderful"—any such thing. For thus he has shown what would be travestied were it to be told.

Introducing the Flood Editions *Selected Poems* (2011), his choice of Fisher's work for an American audience, August Kleinzahler performed the impressive balancing act of both explaining how Fisher "has never aspired to a readership" while asserting that his "selection should broaden Fisher's American readership beyond those very few who have attended to any signs of life in British poetry over the past fifty years." Looked at from a British point of view, the idea that he is and has been a poet discovering what it is possible to do "freed from readership" is perhaps less evidenced than it may be in the United States. Kleinzahler reports Fisher saying that experience of being read helped to precipitate a writing block that let him to release a first *Collected Poems* in the late 1960s while under the impression that his poetry writing days were over.

Yet that experience, and the differently testing one of finding himself polemically misunderstood by Donald Davie in *Thomas Hardy and British Poetry* (1973), did not prevent him from finding imaginative ways beyond these challenges, for finding that he had still not "run out of road". Fisher's sense of his own distinctiveness, his bewilderment, his need to de-socialise his material in order to find artistic value in it, have not in any sense reduced his perceptiveness about what he calls in his self-review "the only world, into which everybody's born already swimming or going under." This is also the 'One World' of a poem in which, sinking or swimming, the children of its lines are simultaneously in the world of the magazine in which the poem was first published and yet, it also acknowledges, unlikely to find themselves reading it:

> But to name names: if John Snook,
> Ann Pouney or Brian Davidson,
> Pat Aston or Royston Williams
> should of their own accord and unprompted
> read over this and remember me—well
> if they're offended they can tell me about it.
> It would be good to know
> we all look at the same magazines.

"I want to believe I live in a single world", Fisher had written at the start of the closing prose paragraph to *City*. The evidence of his occasional prose does suggest that he has both continued to "want to believe" and has been exercised by the degree of discontinuous complexity that this singular entity may contain.

Writing to get around in his mind, "to go on shamanic mental trips though humdrum-looking material", he has also treated himself as a terra incognita, surely the most sensible way to take an interest in one's experience of life, and a further reason why solipsism doesn't seem right, unless to add that he can be solipsistic in his engagement with his supposed solipsism, or, as I would prefer, that his critical detachment even from his own self-absorption lets in the vital glimpses of unexpectedly shared realities that, in my experience, is one of the most lasting and portable values in his writings. Fisher has described himself as "eminently quotable, if only anybody could find a reason to quote him", but he also indicates what such a reason might be in 'Diversions' when "*The power of dead imaginings to return*" is characterized as "Built for quoting in a tight corner." If your troubles lean, as 'The Lesson in Composition' puts it "to the vague and hard-to-help", Fisher's accesses to his "shadowy synesthesia" can prove efficaciously quotable.

Those who have found or have yet to find Roy Fisher's writings can be helped around its corners by growing more familiar with the mental and actual environment, the nurture, as it were, from which they sprang. And since that double-character environment, the world with another one sewn into its lining, has issued in works with such unique natures, any track-ways and signposts will likely prove essential aids to those ramblers who, "of their own accord and unprompted", choose to stray therein.

Note on the Text

This selection from Roy Fisher's occasional prose was organized and shaped by its editor in consultation with the poet. For those curious to note what has been left out, a complete checklist by Derek Slade is provided at the back of the book. In sequencing the items with Fisher's help and advice, I have tried to respect his scepticism about chronology and autobiography, while also offering an ordering of pieces that makes a coherent read through Fisher's recurrent concerns and points of reference. Again, for those who would like to follow the chronology of composition for these pieces, the dates of first publication for most of them are available in the checklist, a listing that also functions as an acknowledgement of the publications and their editors that usually occasioned their writing. One unpublished piece has a more convoluted genesis. 'Concerning Joseph Brodsky' began as a series of responses to generic questions put to Fisher, and a number of other poets in 1997, by Valentina Polukhina. From the raw materials of his answers, and with the blessing of the poet, I have lightly edited them into a series of numbered observations.

The collection has been organized for convenience into three sections: the first contains works related to Fisher's background and environment in twentieth-century Birmingham, his life as a semi-professional jazz pianist, and some memoirs of his life and contacts as a poet; the second brings together writings on his own poetic work and the occasional prefatory notes or commentaries he has written about the composition of individual texts; the third gathers his writings on other jazz pianists, a painter contemporary, a photographer, two novelists, and a range of other poets' works. Some semblance of chronology has been given to all three of these sections, but it is usually one related to the materials, topics, and artists he addresses, not that of the pieces' composition.

The choice of the book's main title is Roy Fisher's, and I have placed the 2012 memoir 'Meanwhile', whose first sentence provides it, at the head of the first section for this reason.

I would like to thank warmly Eleanor Cooke, Roy Fisher, Tony Frazer, Andrew Houwen, and Derek Slade for their help in bringing together the items gathered here. David Prentice agreed before his death to allow one of his works to grace the cover, and I am grateful to his widow for the permission to reproduce. The choice of dedicatee for the book is also Roy Fisher's, and I would like to thank him further for his patience and understanding during the time it has taken to bring this project to completion.

Peter Robinson
June 2014

I

ANTEBIOGRAPHY

MEANWHILE

An easily bewildered child, I nevertheless had no problem in hanging on to the idea that sewn like a lining inside the customary world there was another with tones and imperatives of its own. A shadowy synaesthesia, I suppose, it has been with me lifelong. It visits most days. It arrived without language, for it never came up in conversation, so throughout childhood I drew and painted obsessively, eventually acquiring an identity as the official artist of Wattville Road Junior Elementary School, Handsworth, Birmingham.

A few sharp incursions of language. At about nine, clear-eyed Edna Barnes who sat a few rows in front stood up to sing a song to the class: 'Barbara Allen': words that held beauty, life and death. Around the same time I wrote an epic, 'The Battle of Crécy', in eight thumping lines. Then at twelve, in the grip of a fervent undeclared adulation, I wrote a love poem, a bundle of clichés I was fortunately too timid to deliver. Instead I gave it to a friend to use as valentine to a different girl, substituting her name, at some cost to the metre. I could have charged him a permission fee.

My painting ran out of road, just as I was suddenly hit hard by jazz music, first in the form of the recordings of Chicagoan blues and boogie pianists. Here were sounds from another world: a music in which I was not only permitted but *required* to invent material that resembled my inner existence. Starting from scratch I set myself to learn to play and within a few years had a new identity as a useful jazz club pianist. And alongside that there was a substance called Modern Poetry, which came partly by way of school, where I was studying poetry without any thought of writing it. Young masters back from the war, their tastes formed in the Thirties, would entertain us with oddities by MacNeice and Auden. Much of this poetry was freakish and permissive in a way that took my fancy—Edith Sitwell's obtuse 'Aubade', Pound, some imagists. On my own I'd seek out anthologies of translated poetry from many different ages and cultures; and constantly to hand there was D. B. Wyndham Lewis's *The Stuffed Owl*, a treasury of pretentious and ludicrous verse.

In 1948, in my first year reading English at Birmingham University I became aware that there was a scattering of people who were openly writing and circulating poetry, something I'd never encountered before. There was a staff-student Writers' Circle, and the university's little catch-all arts magazine *Mermaid* always carried a few poems. At the same time my piano-playing had struck a technical *impasse* I couldn't resolve, and the scene that had supported it was tired and in dispersal; so I gave up playing in public for several years. I had a hunch that poetry might hold the sort of energy and surprise I'd been used to finding in music and I began to try building my habitual verbal doodles into poems. My extra-curricular reading was heady and thrill-seeking—Rimbaud, Lautréamont, Dylan Thomas, Dalí, The New Apocalypse, any surrealism I could find—but my own writings turned out spurious, forced and lumpy. I was astonished and baffled by how inept I was. Having nothing to show I made no contacts with the Writers' Circle or the magazine for a couple of years. But I was being trained to write balanced and reasoned critical essays stiffened with whatever flashy-looking erudition I could cadge. I took some of this material, cast it into iambic pentameters and showed the results around. Riding the pentameters was fun though I could sense something hollow and showy; but I was immediately accorded a new identity, as a poet, and was given *Mermaid* to edit. My long hair and bow-tie were justified. At the same time I became fascinated by some, at least, of the ideas in Graves's *The White Goddess*, chiefly its archaic exoticism and the exalted qualities it attributed to poetry. This allegiance had one beneficial effect: it ensured that whatever I wrote during the next five or six years was automatically unpublishable. Meanwhile I learned to write.

A single grotesque fantasy found its way into print, a couple of years after I'd written it, and it caught the eye of Gael Turnbull who was guest-editing a British number of the American magazine *Origin* and on the lookout for anything unusual. We met, and, although his work and mine had little in common, became fast friends for the rest of Gael's life, nearly fifty years. For the first ten of those years all the circulation and acceptance my work had was attributable directly or indirectly to Gael. He opened things up and licensed me to go on writing. Trying to characterize the unique nature of his presence in the poetry scene I'm reminded of the stratified social system of Imperial Japan, where the rigid levels of aristocracy and peasantry held sandwiched between them the Floating World of administrators, artists and the like who had fewer obligations and more freedom. Having virtually no contact with the poetry establishment (particularly in England, though America and eventually his native Scotland found him easier to value) and instinctively staying clear of the activities of self-congratulatory but incurious amateurism, he could roam free in the floating world of little magazines and quixotic publications. He had a nose for what he considered honest work and had no preconceptions about where to go looking for it. He distrusted anything smooth, slick or subsidised: his predilection for issuing tiny editions, mostly of his own work, in booklets hand-sewn with covers of wallpaper offcuts, the texts on the poorest quality paper and made with obsolete basic technology, was proverbial. Some of these qualities were carried forward into the magazine *Migrant*, in fact more a serial anthology of the editors' finds than a conventional magazine, which he set up with Michael Shayer, and then into their Migrant Press, which was to publish my first pamphlet, *City*. Unobtrusively and with no thought of advantage to himself he was the enabler of countless fertile contacts. Stuart Mills, whose Tarasque Press generated several of my pamphlets, was sent to me by Gael as was Stuart Montgomery, founder of Fulcrum Press, which published my first four books.

Antebiography

I must have been conceived during those days in late 1929 when Wall Street was falling in ruins; I was a latecomer in a poor but prudent family which thought itself complete, and although nobody ever hinted as much to me, I can see now that my birth, in June 1930, will have been accompanied by a revival of economic fear and some privation. These were to last until the arrival of the prosperity which the war of 1939 brought to working people. My father was a craftsman, working for the same small, paternalist jewellery firm ("Walter, you're a good workman, and if you ever leave here I'll see to it that you never get another job anywhere in this trade") to which he'd been apprenticed at fourteen, in 1903. It was a luxury trade which withered with the Depression and took a long while to recover; my father was to earn far better wages when the war came, but for assembling aircraft, not setting diamonds. The fact that he then felt it demeaning to become for a while just another factory worker, even for three times the pay, tells something about the family ethos.

Not that he actually enjoyed making jewellery, even though he did take a certain pride in his minute skill: he was in it only because he had been put to it as a boy. Jewellery of some sort had been the family trade for at least three generations; they'd lived in a succession of homes never more than walking distance from the same nest of small workshops just outside the city centre. This was the Jewellery Quarter, a congested patch maybe three quarters of a mile square on the crest of Hockley Hill. It was the archetype, almost a concentrate, of the Birmingham system of proliferating small manufactories which developed through the eighteenth and nineteenth centuries. The "masters" would start by having their workshops attached to their houses, all over the district; the workshops would extend piecemeal to cram the backyards, then the gardens. At that stage the master would move his family a mile or two out to a new suburb, and every room of the original house would be filled with workbenches or clerks' desks. There were hundreds of these establishments in Hockley, dark and chaotic, their work spaces linked by rickety stairways and catwalks. It was an area I saw for the first time only in my teens, working as a telegram delivery boy one school holiday; certainly my father never saw any reason to take me there, and although I once called at W. H. Small's front office with a message when he was in hospital, I never set eyes on the room where, apart from the two wars, he spent every working day for over fifty years. It's quite likely that my mother never learned exactly where the place was.

I think my father would probably have been better suited by temperament to some sort of clerical, white-collar job; he was certainly literate enough. But that would have meant, under the crazy but insidiously effective English system, changing social classes; and for the large family of my grandfather (also Walter Fisher) the game was one of consolidation rather than movement upward. Nobody was put to an education involving expense which future fortune might or might not repay; that would be the plan for my own generation, once the consolidation had taken effect. That family—Lizzie, Ern, Wal, Doris, Jessie, Rose, Albert, Florrie—earned their livings early. My uncle Ern was the only one ever to become his own boss, and that was in a very small way, as half of a two-man japanning business he ran in partnership with his sister Florrie's husband, Will, but which neither of them owned.

I write of that household as being my grandfather's partly as a fact of memory, for my grandmother was dead three years before I was born; but by every account, the setup had always been patriarchal, right from the elder Walter's marriage in 1885, at nineteen (twenty-one on the marriage lines), to Mary Jane Kite. She was two years older, living a few doors away in James Street, Lozells, and on the point of giving birth to my Aunt Lizzie. When I came to know him—or rather to witness him, for he didn't have much interest in children—he was an impressive old man, bald, lean, and hard, with a down-turned moustache and an outfit that included polished leather leggings and made him look more like a shepherd or a stockman dressed up for market day than a man who had spent all his life within a couple of miles of the centre of Birmingham. He was a little bowed, but loping and agile. He stank of tobacco smoke, and his speech was a direct, articulate Old Brummagem, a strong, railing accent, very different from the sodden and nondescript English usually thought of nowadays as the local language. Just by his presence he dominated any room he was in, though I don't remember him as interacting with other people much; for his last ten years or so he was accompanied everywhere by his retriever, which both served as an intimate and did all his socialising for him. You could make contact with him via the dog; and he'd usually give the children a few of the dog's chocolate drops, when the dog had had enough. I was brought up to think of him as something of a household tyrant and a miser, and there was probably some truth in both. He certainly had an unusually large amount of savings for a retired working man who had raised a big family: when he died in 1945 he left over a thousand pounds, enough to buy outright a couple of houses of the sort we were then living in for a rent of ten shillings a week.

He never moved from the house, 77 Anglesey Street, Lozells, in which he'd spent most of his adult life. It was a plain brick street of terrace houses, without bay windows or front gardens, and it ran down from the Lozells Road, which was something of a shopping street, into the factory-filled valley east of Hockley; beyond that, the hill rose by way of Great King Street, where he'd been born, to the Jewellery Quarter, where he worked. In the other direction, away from the city centre, he would in his earlier years have come quickly into open country; and that was the clue to the other side of his life. At the time of his birth, Great King Street will have been almost at the edge of the built-up area, and the other places he lived in—all within a square half-mile or so of one another—were in the zone to which the edge of town had pushed itself by the time he married; James Street looked out into farmland. Once he was settled in Anglesey Street, the suburbs went on spreading beyond him, a good ten miles more, till they almost met, as they now do meet, Walsall, the next town. He didn't, however, do what many small householders did, his own father among them: cultivate his backyard and an allotment garden as well. Although a complete product of the city and its economy, he didn't at all, as far as I know, use the city, and feed off its atmospheres and opportunities in the way really urbanised people do. Whenever he could, he got out.

As he was exactly of the generation of working men who were liberated by the safety bicycle back into the countryside from which their parents or grandparents had probably come. He took his holidays and weekend excursions in male company or alone, by bicycle, covering considerable distances. And the machines he rode were the only extravagance he had. He would have them built to his specifications: not racers, but well-engineered, rugged road cycles. The last of them came to my father as a premature legacy, and quickly to me; it was so heavily constructed that the old man could hardly move it. I found it hard work, too: a smooth, black brute with a broad, sprung saddle, oil-bath chain guard and so much equipment of one sort and another slung low on its bodywork that it would almost stand up by itself.

As he grew older he restricted himself more and more to an old haunt nearer town, the wide stretch of protected wild heath and woodland called Sutton Park, in Sutton Coldfield. He would get away through the suburbs into that. He had been a noted swimmer in the pools there, particularly in the depths of winter, belonging to a group of ice-breaking swimmers; their successors probably still swim for the Walter Fisher Cup, a winter trophy. And it was in that park that he met his death, early in 1945. Since the deaths of my aunt Lizzie and her family in an air-raid (this was the incident described in my poem 'The Entertainment of War') he'd become more and more remote and confused; there were perpetual ringing noises in his head. His trouble was probably tinnitus, but the general opinion—which he may have shared—was that he was losing his wits as he approached eighty. He didn't come visiting any more, communicated with people very little, and finally didn't stir from the house, as if in a terminal feebleness. One January day, he disappeared, and the dog with him. Late the next day, and a dozen miles away in Sutton Park, the dog led a passer-by to where he lay dying of exposure after a freezing night. I think everybody considered it a good death for him. Uncle Ern and my father cycled out to the park with his ashes, no doubt strapped to the carrier of his own massive bicycle, and scattered them near Blackroot Pool.

The style of all the Fishers was one of alert, short-range attention; humour was brisk and dismissive, even abrupt. Their voices could be sharp or declamatory, and their movements and facial expressions tended to the vigorous and, on occasion, manic. They coped with life as they went along, and on the level they found themselves on. Constitutionally, they kept their noses clean and a little money in the bank. Of my grandfather's children, none, so far as I know, ever faced insolvency, traumatic unemployment, or breakdown; none engaged in crime; none met with a great increase in fortune, or went looking for such a thing. When they came to have taller, better-educated children, electric light, and indoor lavatories, it was only at the pace at which those things came to many other people. They didn't direct themselves much to the future, and spent little time reminiscing—mostly, I think, because the past had been so harsh they didn't enjoy thinking about it. Of my grandfather's numerous brothers and sisters, for instance, I only ever heard one talked about, and that in long retrospect. This was Great-Uncle John, who was uncharacteristic. Born in 1859, he made the move away from manual work two generations early, becoming the first qualified "high-speed typewriter" in Birmingham. He then married into a Catholic family; his wife was judged to have been a woman of some pretensions; and on her he begot, it was said, three headmistresses. Dominated by his womenfolk, he became eccentrically speculative, and would happily give his money away; I suppose he was a steady hypomanic. At any rate, his family consigned him to institutions from time to time. But for the rest, virtually everything I know about them from the time before I was born comes not from anecdote but from searching the public records. In 1861, my great grandfather William Fisher, an electroplater (probably working in the bulkier end of the jewellery trade) was recorded as living in Great King Street with his wife, Georgina Mason, and their six children (and there were more to come, including my grandfather) in a household headed by her mother, a widow born in Hornton in Oxfordshire and working as a mangler. The Kites and the other tributary family, the Mousleys, were almost certainly already in the same parish somewhere. Ann Mason and her husband had arrived in the city around 1825, to work as button-makers. Both came from families settled as far back as records go—to around 1600—in a tight clutch of villages in the rolling country around Edge Hill: Avon Dassett, Burton Dassett, Hornton, Fenny Compton. Unvaryingly, the occupations had been in or close to farming, with a slow decline in status and possessions.

I never heard of any of the Fishers having any political allegiance, nor any trace of felt religion. My father would describe his father as having been a Freethinker, but I think that just meant he was a sceptic. There exist photographs of my father and his brother Ern as young men, in a Methodist cricket team; there are also photographs of them, from the same period, in a Church of England football eleven. My father also passed the most exalted period of his life as a boy chorister at that same church. The religion seemed to have no effect on him, but socially the church choir affected him a good deal. For one thing, it came close to removing him from his family, from his class, and from Birmingham. That was when, as head chorister and principal soloist, he was talent-spotted for the choir of Canterbury Cathedral with, I suppose, the offer of a free scholarship to the Cathedral Choir School and all the opportunities for social mobility that would carry with it. For some reason, my grandfather didn't give his consent; the refusal wasn't thought to be out of character. At any rate, my father stayed on at Saint Mary's, Handsworth, for as long as his voice lasted, and beyond: far from being eager to drop his register and come out as a man, he wanted to preserve his position, and the excitement of singing the high line, long past the natural time. He forced his voice to stay up till it was a falsetto, probably ruining any prospect of having a reasonable adult singing voice. He certainly never acquired anything more than a rather strained tenor, and as a man didn't sing much. In a rare moment of reminiscence he once gave me the best possible summary of his relationship with my grandfather. "I only ever heard my father sing once," he said; "I came home early, and as I came up the entry I heard a man singing in a most beautiful tenor voice. And that was my dad. And when he heard me he stopped, and then pretended he hadn't been doing it. I never heard him do it again."

Saint Mary's choir was an interesting choice. Handsworth was then an altogether leafier and more affluent place than Lozells, and Saint Mary's was several churches away from my father's home territory. He must have been drawn there by an ambition to sing in the strongest team. The church was the handsome medieval parish church of an independent Staffordshire borough, not annexed by Birmingham till 1911, and at that time one of the districts where the manufacturers had their mansions and the clerical and business classes their villas. It was a place of parlour maids and tennis courts, and the quality came to church in carriages. The church itself had numerous clergy, a huge choir, and was a centre of social power; at the same time it had—as it still has—something of the atmosphere of a village church, sandstone-built and set in a spacious graveyard under a canopy of tall trees. It embodied the English tradition which the industrial nineteenth century was reaching for, inventing where necessary and taking to itself as a talisman; and I'm sure its sub-Gothic dignities had a strong and romantic effect on my father's imagination. It didn't prompt him to social climbing, but was more of an escapism, allied to the old man's cycle rides, which he often shared.

One of the local girls who sat in the front pew and made eyes at the choirboys was a jobbing gardener's daughter called Emma—or Pem, the only person I've ever heard of with that name—Jones. Their courtship turned out to be long: they were married in Saint Mary's in the autumn of 1918, by which time she was twenty-seven and my father twenty-nine, a signals lance-corporal in the London Fusiliers on leave from France. But my father's careful pencil drawing of the church was already in her autograph album by the time he was a sixteen-year-old jeweller's apprentice and boy soprano and she was just starting work in a small sweetshop in the area everybody called "the village," the group of shops round the old toll bar in Villa Road, about midway between her family territory and his.

Whereas the Fishers seem to have been established on their small patch for generations, the Joneses were new arrivals in Handsworth. They'd lived for a time near Harborne, further round the semi-rural western edge of the city, and my grandfather Edward Jones had at some time worked for the Chamberlain family: possibly Joseph, the creator of the modern Birmingham; certainly Austen, who became Foreign Secretary. My grandmother Emma Westwood had had some family connection with a laundry business and had done housekeeping work in one of the smaller outlying hospitals; I have the impression that she'd also been in domestic service. Something of that sort was certainly the family style, which was in marked contrast to that of the Fishers; the contrast was worked out year after year in the household I grew up in, and it made an uncomfortable inheritance. The Joneses had the air of servants who'd been paid off, given their freedom, and who weren't too happy with the bargain; life was an ache, a trial to be faced with cheerfulness and charm amid slowly declining fortunes. I don't know whether this air of decline was based in anything substantial. The Joneses didn't reminisce any more than did the Fishers; and although their thoughts seemed to be turned towards the past, they were thoughts that lay too deep for tears, or words. Usually, at any rate; I can remember seeing my mother and my aunts weeping for times gone by. And there was always something wistful about the charm and the cheerfulness. There was certainly nothing of the bluff pugnacity of the Fishers.

This was, of course, the mood I learned to know in the thirties, and it may be that the one focus of reminiscence and overt regret which they had was the real cause of the pervading wistfulness. This was the loss of Ivy Cottage, something which happened quite a few years before I was born. Somehow, on arriving in Handsworth around the turn of the century, the family had gained the tenancy of an idyllic old yeoman cottage, left marooned in woodland and among fields as the prosperous suburb developed all round it; and there they seem to have lived an almost rural life for a quarter of a century. In speech and manner they gave the impression of being country people, and by preserving that style for so long within a couple of miles of the city centre, they seemed also to be preserving a pre-industrial past. It was only when they lost Ivy Cottage— the story went that they were in some way tricked out of the lease—that they had to become urbanised. Even so, Howard Road, to which they had moved by the time I was born, was far from being a harsh city street. It was a quiet little cut-through, with varied housing, mostly quite old, and a small farmhouse and yard still tucked away behind the houses. But Ivy Cottage had been a complete survival, with climbing roses, old brickwork, and a pump in the yard. It sat among its birch trees half a mile or so up beyond Saint Mary's, and I suppose that for my father it was a powerful additional magic to be added to whatever the church gave him.

The other contrast to the life he was used to lay in the fact that the Jones family was emphatically matriarchal. My soulful-eyed grandmother ran things, persuasively and without resistance. She did it mostly from her bed in later years. My grandfather Edward Jones I knew as a slow, sweet-natured old man, white-bearded, straw-hatted, and with distant blue eyes:

the type-figure of a retired gardener. I was told he'd been perhaps a little less uncomplicated in earlier years, before a fall through a hothouse roof and a crack on the head; there was no knowing. He outlived my grandmother by ten years, but didn't liberate himself from his chimney-corner existence.

The family wasn't a matriarchy of the strong sort where daughters breed daughters and men are peripheral; it was a home base near the end of a line, and it exerted a steady, soft, sweet magnetism. When my mother used the word "home" we knew that she meant—although she'd never lived in it—her parents' house in Howard Road. My grandparents had five children, four of whom lived to adulthood, and of those four only my mother married and had children. Her elder sister Elsie worked from home as a dressmaker to the local well-to-do, and became, when past child-bearing, the third wife of an elderly *rentier* who lived opposite, enjoying, while she lasted, the slight elevation of position which had come to her by way of a little patience. My mother herself was to marry quite late. Uncle Ted, a bighearted, affectionate bachelor, who worked as a builder's labourer, died in his middle forties, a few months after his mother. The youngest, Ethel, born in 1900, was by general agreement pampered and brought up to idleness, after which she spent thirty years or so keeping house for her parents till they died. She went out to work, cleaning and then doing light factory work, only when she was near retiring age; she never married.

I've said that the contrast between the styles of the Fishers and the Joneses made for an uncomfortable inheritance. On the credit side, the Joneses' quasi-rural nostalgia combined with my father's inherited commitment to country excursions to provide, through my childhood, blissful, almost visionary experiences on outings and walks, supported by an unshakable moral faith in something called Nature. That basic guidance, and many of those experiences have stayed with me all my life. There are people who know me for my writings about urban landscapes and city life and who find it impossible to square that knowledge with the fact that I now live, not as a lifelong denizen of those streets, but in a quite remote and wild place in the Derbyshire hills. But it's the paradox I was given as a child— the sensation of having been born in a state of exile from some unknown countryside—which forced me to stare so hard at all the particulars of my city surroundings.

The real discomfort was social, a matter of loyalties and emotional allegiances. My father was probably the least matter-of-fact, the most reflective of the Fishers; he would need to be, to marry into the Jones family, into which he fitted quite well, though as the years went by, he grew impatient and dismissive about what he considered their passivity, and the uselessness of their little bits of gentility. By the time I was born he probably saw much more of my mother's family than he did of his own. We children certainly did. Visits to Grandpa Fisher's house in Anglesey Street came once or twice a year, so that it felt physically like a foreign territory, whereas the Jones house in Howard Road was a home from home, visited on many weekends and filled with familiar objects and sensations. Being brought up close to my mother—and she was by nature possessive of her two sons—I absorbed, without explicit teaching, the very strong sense that the Jones way was the true way, and that the Fisher way was the way of a heartless world with no leaves on the trees, no flowers in the vases, and sharp edges everywhere. There was no enmity between the families—simply the assumption, from my mother's side, of an inherent incompatibility. And when my parents were at odds, usually about money, the incompatibility of the clans became personal: my father was characterised as a hot-tempered miser, my mother as a devious and indulgent spendthrift. These were just the positions they repeatedly took up; the money there was to argue over was pathetically little. But the slogans of those occasional wars made their impression on me.

My mother was thirty-nine and my father forty-one when I was born. And for our sort of people those were advanced ages for childbearing. My sister was ten years, and my brother eight years my senior; and my parents seemed much older in relation to me than did those of other children. My mother, for instance, was prematurely grey: I never knew her with dark hair. And my father was bald, with nothing boyish about his demeanour. And I came to realise—though not really until I reached that time of life myself— that they were both by then in quite poor shape and had their troubles. They did well to be as animated as they were. I don't think for instance, that giving me birth had done my mother any good at all. She didn't always walk well, couldn't go up or down stairs except one step at a time, and already had the beginnings of a tremor which plagued her later years.

As for my father, I think now that he was an uncompensated war casualty. After volunteering, being rejected as unfit because of a cartilage injury, and undergoing surgery to make himself eligible for service, he spent three years in the trenches, an experience about which he had little to say. He didn't set any value on it, or on his campaign medals or on the results of the Allies' victory. Physically, he was a fairly small man, and I imagine he must always have been nervous, tensed like a spring; on the football field he'd been a fast wing forward, and at cricket a ferociously fast bowler. The stress of his war service, and the problems and frustrations which followed it, will have damaged him. By the time I knew him, there was not an atom of relaxation in him, most of the time. He'd continued with his sports past the age when it would have been sensible to stop, and had pushed himself too far. He was in frequent pain from rheumatism and stomach ulcers, and he slept badly. His thyroid had become seriously over-active and he repeatedly refused the surgery which was the only available treatment. He was hard for a child to get to know; much of what I thought of as his personality, the signs I read him by, must have been the phenomenology of his illness: the losses of temper, the over-loud laughter, the friendliness that seemed far more forced and uneasy than it was. It alarmed me, I suppose, and distanced me from him, and it never occurred to me to model my behaviour on his in any way. When I took to doing things I'd learned from him, like roaming the countryside, on foot or bicycle, I arrogantly assumed I was doing it my way; and it was with real astonishment that I discovered, in adulthood, that it was his face I'd inherited more than my mother's. I'd ruled out any such possibility.

It's easy for me to see my whole character, and the course of my life, as determined by an early disposition to be, quietly and without fuss, as unlike him as possible in the way I did things. Where he was keen, quick and hyperactive, I grew up to be laid back, non-committal, sceptical about the value of any action at all. This scepticism was strengthened by the spectacle of the fascinating but turbulent adolescent years of my sister and brother.

And I grew secretive. This wasn't purely temperamental. Either parent would sound me out about what the other might be thinking or doing. I didn't like that; but it taught me that the discovery of others' plans, motives, and feelings was a powerful currency. In consequence, I became disinclined fully to confide anything in anybody, a habit which was to stay with me long after it was of any possible tactical use. A few years ago I made a note: "My life is the history of my secrets." Which meant, not that my secrets ever amounted to anything, but that my whole sense of myself was as a carrier of secrets. Early on, I'd decided that if secrets spelled safety, the best course for me was to be a secret incarnate. Good for the contemplative life, if in a warped way; bad for the active.

And when the active life hit me, when I went at five to Wattville Road School, I was unprepared for it. I'd had the upbringing many youngest children receive, being capably but unconcernedly looked after by an experienced mother who was busy with the still-unfamiliar challenges generated by the older children. I was just kept close to my mother; the other people I met for five years were mostly relatives, and mostly adults. I had very little contact with other children. So my first day at school, when I suddenly encountered what felt like the whole of the rest of the human race, was a shock. I still haven't got over it. Something had got at all those children and brutalised them. They were loud and aggressive—even their friendliness was intrusive—and they were even more taboo-ridden than I was. Even when they didn't seem intelligent, they behaved as if far more worldly-wise than me. Since I was never worldly-wise, and not rebellious in an active way, I was always to be puzzled by the way the world seemed to run on taboos and bans, a life defined by its negatives. My parents, without any theology beyond a sentimental attachment to the church where they'd met, often seemed to have devised a secular Calvinism, overhung with calamity to come, a calamity in and of the world.

I hated school, apart from one or two encouraging relationships with teachers when I was ten or eleven, and I learned to survive in a paradoxical way—I soon found out that I was better than most, if not all, of the others at the lessons; and I could sing and draw, though I'm left-handed and writing was an agony, particularly with steel pens and filthy ink. I had no talent for naughtiness, and so had all the qualifications of a teacher's pet. Insofar as I wanted to, I could always have a secure place close to the seat of authority, crazy as that authority might seem. At the same time, I had no standing in the playground, a place which always seemed to me a chaos of violence and spite. Out there, I was for years "the Daft Kid," the slow-on-the-uptake, the dim-witted. And since that was my name, that was who I believed I was. The knowledge that I always beat them all at schoolwork was a palliative, but no more. They were reality, after all. I was never without friends, but they were drawn from the quieter end of the mob. The rougher end was something to worry about: it had some wild and violent characters from down beyond the railway tracks, and I came to rely on my acquired persona as a talisman for physical safety—"Let him alone, he's only the Daft Kid."

The railway line was a real, as well as a notional, boundary in the patch of ground where I grew up—a landmark which was in fact made by its shape and the uses it had in those days, into a moralized landscape. That edge of Handsworth is an easy slope running down from the ridge carrying the Birmingham-Holyhead road and into Winson Green and Smethwick, at whose conjunction Matthew Boulton's Soho Foundry stood. Wattville

Road (there never was a place called Wattville, though it may once have been projected) is a straight track from top to bottom of that slope, with the main railway line which leads north-west out of the city centre three miles away crossing it halfway down; the school is the last thing before the railway bridge as you go down. The zone above the railway was mainly given over to streets of fairly tidy terraced houses; these included Kentish Road, where I was born and lived until I was twenty-three. And up beyond those streets were newer houses, a park, sports grounds, a huge semi-rural municipal cemetery, and a patch of farmland. But below the railway, the hill seemed to steepen, dropping among slum houses to a valley bottom filled with all the gigantic signs of heavy industry: chimney stacks, black and rusting factory buildings, huge gas-holders, a pandemonium of metallic noise, a network of oily, green canals. The whole place was threatening, harsh, and mysterious. Also it was a zone to which we had no entrée, since my father worked a good way nearer town, in the Jewellery Quarter.

We were out there on the western edge of Handsworth by way of a temporary expedient which turned permanent. When my father came out of the army in 1919, he and my mother, then pregnant, lodged in the house, 74 Kentish Road, rented by his sister Lizzie and her husband. It was well away from either Jones or Fisher territory. Before long, Lizzie's family moved, first to a house in the same street, then eventually to the house down on the edge of Smethwick, where they were all to be killed twenty years later. My parents took on the tenancy of 74; their three children were born there and they themselves stayed there till they died, my father in 1959 and my mother in 1965.

Kentish Road was in a small edge-of-town development of four uniform terraced streets, built some time between 1900 and 1910. Originally they had backed onto pasture-land, but that had been taken over by the sports field and timber yard of the Birmingham Carriage and Wagon Company, whose main gate was at the bottom of our street and whose territory occupied the whole of the southern outlook from our backyard. It made a decent, docile, politically conservative working-class district which at that time showed hardly anything of the raw impulse towards affluence which was to drive almost all the inhabitants to flee from it in the fifties. When I was a child, many of the adults around me had been born in vile slums; it was as if they were resting for a generation before moving on. It was a quiet, tired, fatalistic place, where the people made great efforts to establish and guard their privacy. There was very little of the proverbial working-class habit of being always in and out of one another's houses.

Our house was small, though I've lived in bigger ones that felt smaller. It had a tiny garden at the front, with a domed bush of yellow privet and a border of bluebells. There was a narrow hall, and a front parlour with a piano and an archaic three-piece suite. The living room had a deal table with a green chenille cloth, a black-leaded range, again with a chenille valance round its high mantelpiece, on which stood a polished brass shell-case and other ornaments. There was an old blue basket chair, and the remains of a suite upholstered in green and red. Down one step was the narrow little kitchen containing a stone sink with the house's one tap, a built-in copper boiler, a small range fireplace, a black gas cooker, a mangle that folded to make a table, and, in wet weather, my father's and my brother's bicycles. There was a canary in a cage, my father's pet; and outside in the blue-brick-paved yard he had others—fish in an aquarium on a stand, and a large wall-mounted cage for a song thrush. Along the yard were a coal house and a toilet with a scrubbed plank seat. The house was a set of closed compartments, in which it was possible for the five of us to have some seclusion from one another when we wanted it, if not from the neighbours, whose noise came through the walls on either side regardless. The staircase was hidden behind a door opening off the living room and led to three bedrooms, one very small. The house was lit, rather dimly, by gas, except for the bedrooms, where, since the gas was unreliable, we burned oil. I had a home-made lamp made from a coffee bottle filled with paraffin, with a bootlace for a wick. The whole place was floored with cold linoleum, and there were a couple of home-made rag hearth rugs. There were few books, and we took a newspaper and comics; there were some intensely memorable monochrome framed prints, and four gilt-framed original oil paintings by a local artist; I still have three of them. Nothing much changed in the house till the end of the thirties, when an upturn in the jewellery trade and, probably more significantly, the fact that my sister and brother had left school and were earning, brought electric light and some more modern furniture.

The gardens were the width of the houses, ten or twelve feet, and no more than thirty feet long: they were strips for hanging out washing. My father took ours over and populated it densely with plants and animals. Against the solid sports-field fence he improvised a shed for hens and rabbits; the other fences he raised to head-height with scrap wood from fruit crates and covered them with rambler roses; all the rest of the space was crammed with cottage garden flowers and whatever vegetables there was room for. Beyond the garden, the chief amenity was open sky. The sports field, much of it rough grass, stretched away for half a mile, with the next factory buildings miniaturised beyond it; and to the left, the works timber yard was spacious and remote, with a small locomotive and a couple of steam cranes puffing about in it. I always had one of the bedrooms facing out westwards over this area; there was nothing claustrophobic about being there.

That open view was important. Even more so was the access to the area of countryside which opened up ten minutes' walk away, across the Holyhead road. Although it lay at the city boundary it wasn't open country; that was a couple of hours' bus ride away. The few square miles of land we had, a single shallow valley under a crest of upland, was just a patch that hadn't yet been turned to city uses, lying across the widening stretch between that Holyhead road and the next one to the east, that went on to Stafford and Manchester. The Birmingham suburbs petered out just about where we lived, and gave way to this rather run-down bit of country, which, strangely, didn't go on reaching to the north-west as the roads diverged, but was hemmed in after a few miles by a string of industrial townships which gradually joined up to isolate it. But it was an enclosure whose edges you didn't have to think about, unless you wanted to react to the mysterious sight of sunlit cooling towers rising above a misty horizon ten miles away. It was a vista of fields and copses and rags of hedgerow, stands of tall trees, and the long sandstone wall of what had been the Earl of Dartmouth's estate. Its heart was made up of five or six farms, dominated by a pair of collieries; a railway branch line ran through the fields, and pushing quietly in from the edges were the spacious, land-grabbing outreaches of city life; two lonely golf courses with birch woods and scrub; a public park; the vast cemetery, still mostly unused, and, wherever the houses stopped, allotment gardens packed with weird shanties with their flue-pipes, rain-barrels, and bits of pub window.

So there was no clear distinction between the town and the country. The cemetery and the golf course had wild edges to them, and the desolate reed-bordered pool that was the destination for special excursions lay, with a complete scenic rightness, under the arid, black and red-brown spoil heap of Jubilee Colliery, with its baleful flat top and the deep scars of rain channels running down to the thickets of alder and willow around its base. Nobody ever suggested in my hearing that the collieries or the cemetery or the allotments were "spoiling" the landscape. They were part of it; it was a particular type of countryside that had those things in it.

When I was old enough I would spend, with friends or alone, walking or cycling, a great deal of time there. When I was younger it was a regular

Sunday-morning excursion with my father, part of a routine set of activities. We'd walk the lanes while my mother cooked. In the afternoon she'd join us for a strange family party on one of the upper slopes of the cemetery, with sweeping views. A selection of my father's brothers and sisters, their spouses and children—up to a dozen people—would gather at the grave of my grandmother and my Uncle Albert, who'd died young. My grandfather never came. They'd change the flowers in the marble urn, talk for an hour, and disperse. I grew to be quite at home there. When my mother's mother and uncle Ted were buried a couple of hundred yards down the slope, some of us would tend that too. It had a patch of turf, which my father would clip with a pair of kitchen scissors he carried in his pocket.

Sometimes we'd take our walks in the other direction, down into Hell, quiet and sunlit on a Sunday morning. Whereas I took the countryside to be righteous, there was a whiff of addiction about my appetite for the beauty of the great rusting sheds, the tarry stinks, and the slimy canals of Smethwick. It was a lonely and gigantic landscape, with hardly anybody in it.

Until I was in my teens we travelled very little indeed. Each year there'd be a trip or two to the city centre, little more than three miles away, and a day's outing by bus or tram to one of the traditional spots just outside the city—the Lickey Hills, or Kinver Edge. Before I was born, there had been family holidays by the sea, but I was never to go on holiday with my parents. I was thirteen before I slept a night outside Birmingham; and there had probably been only two or three nights away from home in all that time. There were a few day trips to more distant places, so rare and so unreal that they had for me the impact of transcendental spiritual visitations. At six I was taken to the Malverns, and in a neighbour's car to the Vale of Llangollen and the mountains and sea-coast of North Wales. The same neighbours later took us to the Vale of Evesham and Dovedale. These places—I didn't know where they were, or why they were as they were—excited me enormously.

I was already reading obsessively, the books coming not from school, where the provision was thin, but from the public library, which I joined shortly after starting school. And I was drawing. I started with a blackboard and coloured chalks, then went on to cover every paper surface that could be provided for me, usually with pencil and crayon drawings, sometimes with watercolour. I was fairly slapdash, but I don't think I conformed for long to what is expected of child artists. I was inspired by the illustrators of adventure stories, historical romances, and by the appearances of things as I saw them at the cinema. All these I set myself to copy, repeating and developing favourite scenes over and over again. The siege of Omdurman in *The Four Feathers*, and episodes from the Errol Flynn *Robin Hood*, Trafalgar, from *Lady Hamilton*. I drew in a sort of panoramic realism, with scores of characters accurately costumed and equipped, and mostly stuck full of spears or arrows.

For years this activity was the most positive thing in my life. It led to the only real lift I got from my school days, something which should, I suppose, have set me on a career as a painter had I been able to seize the advantage. In September 1939, the school had been closed down and most of the children evacuated to the country. My parents elected not to send me, reasoning on my behalf that, were they to be killed, the double bereavement would be more than I could bear, and that hence I would no doubt prefer to be blown to bits along with them. I was told all this at the time, and was persuaded. Early in 1940, the school reopened for the few who remained, and I quickly passed the examination qualifying me to go on to the grammar school when I was old enough, in a year and a half's time. In doing so, I'd virtually exhausted the Wattville Road curriculum and had time to spare. Pop Lewis, my teacher, a shrewd and spirited Welshman, played a hunch and set me up in a corner with a full-sized blackboard and easel, a set of powder colours and brushes, the biggest sheet of paper I'd ever seen, and a commission to paint *The Knights of the Round Table Asleep under the Hill until Britain's Hour of Need*. It took days, and people came to watch. I rose to the challenge. When the picture was hung high on the classroom wall I had a little fame, and the status of court painter. I was excused lessons for long periods to paint subjects of my choice. My range was wide: *The Last Fight of the 'Revenge', Marco Polo Setting Out from Venice to Asia, Everyday Life in Ancient Rome, Abraham Leading Isaac Away from the Family Tent to Be Sacrificed, Marco Polo Returning to Venice from Asia*. There was even a street scene, painted from the life. These all hung above the desks, a deep, lengthening frieze. I suppose I had talent. I certainly enjoyed my role, and took it seriously.

Outside the painting, however, there were things starting to go wrong for me. At seven I'd become myopic and had to wear glasses. I took this blow very badly, for it removed me overnight from any hope of normality. We were a family accustomed to dark good looks in youth, and I was now not going to make it. As well as being the Daft Kid I had to join the very small number of children who were patronised, or worse, for having some physical disability. Adults were kind; children, boys and girls alike, were merciless, until the novelty wore off. My outer and inner lives started to drift away from each other. Anxiously overfed by my mother, I grew fat, and stayed so. My life started to move in a series of lurches, between mild hope and mild despair. The war itself had a mixed effect. The air raids of 1940, when I spent many of my nights in the Anderson shelter in the garden, with bombs and equally lethal British shrapnel whistling down, were exciting but appalling, not so much from the fear of a notional death as from the actual presence afterwards of acres of destruction and disorder, the still, featureless mountains of bricks which had been neighbouring streets. After that, my brother and my brother-in-law spent years in danger. I would engage in elaborate daily, muttered rituals, which grew longer and longer, in order to ensure their safety, which I believed depended only on me. At the same time, there was, with the prolongation of stoicism, a deadening of areas of feeling.

Moving to Handsworth Grammar School cheered me up at first. Life was socially more comfortable, and the air of tradition—most of it fairly new in fact—was supportive and seductive for a while. But merely being selected to go there, a mile away from home, isolated me to an exaggerated extent from the place I'd grown up in. From my Wattville Road class of forty, only three of us went to the Boys' Grammar School and two or three to the Girls'. Nobody from Kentish Road had ever gone before, except my own sister and brother, years before. This fact, the expectation that all the Fisher children were on the conveyor belt and in the process of being educated out of the street, set the family apart, in an odd way. We weren't brash or go-getting, but there was a slight air of our having received a higher call.

Handsworth Grammar School was a nineteenth-century foundation. Like nearly all such places it had developed the function of educating the sons of local lower-middle-class families—technical, clerical, shopkeeping, the sort of people who didn't send their children away to boarding schools—to perpetuate that class, and in addition to draw promising working-class boys "up" into it. The handful of us from Wattville Road were of the latter sort; certain other schools in better-off neighbourhoods sent their boys to the grammar school *en masse*. The staff was fairly typical, except for its Head, a product of public school and Cambridge, a haughty, cold-mannered zealot, an Anglican cleric and a Buchmanite, whose declared aim was to reproduce, as far as was possible in such a place, the ethos of a public school like Arnold's Rugby. Its application was to be local, to feed industry with technically and scientifically trained personnel, in the process declassing any whose class origins were likely to hamper their social mobility. We were encouraged, for instance, to lose the local characteristics in our speech; with the blood of servants running in my veins, and some talent for mimicry, I turned out to be quite good at this game. The family accent wasn't a strongly-marked Brummagem, but tended to take on different characteristics according to the occupations its speakers followed. I easily acquired a neutral, go-anywhere accent—so easily that I later felt angry at the way it had smoothed out of my memory the speech I first had. I can't hear my own voice.

I soon learned that painting played no part in the school's plans for my advancement. The top stream into which I was put had no art in its curriculum, no examinable music, no geography or history. I let my painting and drawing go without a fight; I couldn't see what the fight could have been. I kept them going as private activities for a while, but the talent didn't survive puberty. By this time, though, I was singing, untrained, in the school choir, having taken to it too late to make the sort of mark my father and brother—who had followed him as head chorister at Saint Mary's, as did my son Joe—had made. Technically I did join that choir, conquering my distaste for the liturgy and the fancy dress, but so late that during a bout of pneumonia that came between my audition and my debut my voice had broken. But it was to be music that first replaced painting for me.

That illness, a couple of months away from the world after passing through mortal danger, was a rite of passage, a Magic Mountain in miniature. I spent most of it in my room, looking out at the sky over the factory yard and the field, watching the spring arrive, reading, drawing, and thinking. My feelings sharpened and clarified. After the confusion and pain of the illness had passed, I was happy in my isolation. I experienced, in fact, many of the sensations of Mann's hero. I was twelve. When I emerged, I was less of a child. I hadn't become a conventional, active adolescent; I lurked behind a vaguely juvenile manner for years. But it was as if I'd been somewhere unknown, and had come back altered. Wherever it was, it's the location of my imagination; it's still the place I have to find in order to write, and its essential qualities never alter. It combines a sense of lyrical remoteness with an apprehension of something turbulent, bulky, and dark. There, I don't have to bother to grow older.

I didn't move towards writing at that time, though I was reading everything I could find—and also listening to the radio. We'd acquired a radio only a little while before the war began, and I spent, like almost everybody else, a great part of the next five years listening to BBC broadcasts indiscriminately. The BBC was still very much as Reith had left it; it was also wartime, and the British, disoriented, had inadvertently dropped some of their defences against experiencing the arts. It was from reading the *Radio Times*, in those days an earnest and responsible journal, that I first realised there was an adult world of music, painting, and writing all around me, out of immediate reach but capable of being sought after. Very gradually, I found my way around. It was late in 1943, when I had the musical tastes of an unassisted thirteen-year-old—I knew all the popular tunes of the day, along with a little Handel, a little Rossini, Tchaikovsky, Holst, Grieg—that I was knocked permanently into a different trajectory by a single record heard on a request programme. This was Meade Lux Lewis' 1936 piano solo, 'Honky Tonk Train Blues'. In the three minutes it took to hear it, it seemed as if every cell I had was mobilised to go in search of those unimagined sounds, which seemed to have nothing to do with any music I'd ever heard—even jazz, which had simply sounded rackety, over-urgent stuff.

In those same minutes, I realised that my new passion was to be yet another of my secrets: nobody would approve of it. I began listening to any programmes where the music might appear, dissembling my intense interest, even joining in the insults it provoked when it showed up. I started scraping away at our semi-derelict piano in an attempt to reproduce what I was hearing, and kept on doing so until I had some success, believing all the while that my ambition was secret. I don't know how I persuaded myself that this could be. The noise, in a small house, was loud, brutal, and insistent; neighbouring shift-workers complained. My parents suggested I should take lessons, probably in the hope that my practice would become more euphonious, but I declined, believing that the lessons would come between me and what I wanted to play—and, by declining, storing up years of technical troubles; I was to reach fifty before I took any lessons.

It wasn't long before my pursuit of piano boogie opened up the whole of jazz. I listened to whatever was broadcast—we had no gramophone—and, almost more important, read whatever there was to read. Two books, Wilder Hobson's *American Jazz Music* and Hugues Panassié's *Le Jazz hot* modelled as they were on orthodox musical criticism and intent on assimilating the new art to the traditional ones, were the first developed writings about any of the arts I ever encountered. I read them over and over again, and can still call whole sentences up from memory. They had an enormous influence on the way I thought in general, and in particular, directed my taste to a congenial quarter, the white Chicago musicians who came up in the twenties and continued to work in association with Eddie Condon—Bud Freeman, Dave Tough, Joe Sullivan, Pee Wee Russell, Jess Stacy. Of all the men who had ever made jazz, these constituted the only group whose circumstances were at all like my own.

The passion for jazz and for the piano was one of the positive lurches. It kept me going through a dreary period of school examinations, and the last stages of the war and its aftermath. By the end of 1943 I'd grown out of feeding off the war in any way, and it had turned to an endless dull horror. I was not cheered by the atomic bomb, or by the manifest state of things as the Cold War set in. My father's brief prosperity ended, and he went back, none too happily, to his jewellery firm. The young men of the family came back, much older and without illusions. At school, I moved up into the vestigial Arts Sixth, without objectives and feeling much further out of my depth than I need have done. There was an undertow of what I can only describe as unfelt sadness, somehow drawing my spirits down, not dramatically but gently and steadily.

Sometime early in 1946 I left the world, and stayed away from it for three years. Afterwards, I found it hard to get back, and I still sometimes experience the recurring shadow of that time. What happened was that I radically revalued the currency of my dealings with my life: I renegotiated my contract. In the quiet madness that took hold of me I became convinced, without any evidence, that I had an unknown, virtually undetectable form of tuberculosis, and was already too far gone for treatment to be of any use. I had two or three years left at the most. I would certainly never see twenty. More to the point, I would never have to.

The disease was then still a common-enough killer of young people, and I'd seen it at work; and I imagine my particular form of hysteria is common enough in the literature—though the only person I've ever known who entertained it, and in an almost identical form, is another poet, Patricia Beer. At all events, I now held the biggest of all my secrets. I was dead. No one must know. The shock would kill my parents, naturally; so delay their learning about it as long as possible. As the possessor of a deadly disease, I also had the power of life and death over everybody I met. I had no inclination to be other than merciful, so for three years I didn't, apart from the odd unavoidable handshake and an arm's-length dandling of my newborn nieces, touch another human being. This was easy. Nobody observed any change in my behaviour, and there probably was none.

I was extremely healthy. In order to guard my secret I didn't go near a doctor for the whole of the period, nor did I need to. I stayed fat, cycled everywhere—while I could, until the unmistakable signs should appear. I kept on reading, coasted through schoolwork, developed my piano playing to the point where I could start appearing in public, sitting in with a band and playing solo spots at local jazz clubs.

Everything, though, was temporary. I put down nothing for the future, prepared nothing, confided in nobody. The renegotiated contract meant that I needed to do nothing beyond dabbling, diverting myself from my awful fate. As for motivation and structure, they were taken care of by the daily business of preserving my cover—for I wanted to remain at large as long as I could get away with it, secure in the knowledge that it wouldn't be for an inconveniently long time. I'd had almost enough of life: I didn't want in, but I didn't want out strongly enough to commit suicide. Indeed, I didn't have the strength of feeling of a suicide.

I structured my life as a spy must—days of low-key activities, offbeat, bitchy humour, casual-seeming appearances here and there, all within the main concern of preserving cover. I did enough work, for instance, to get myself a university place (whatever that might be—I didn't know) simply because attending a university would delay the army medical which would expose me and consign me precipitately to the sanatorium where I would spend my last months in the composition of a few important poems, probably in the style of Matthew Arnold. When I learned that Birmingham University, where my place was, administered a medical to all freshmen, I stayed at school for a further year to try for a scholarship at Cambridge, which, so far as I knew, didn't do anything so intrusive. That step meant that I was made Head Prefect, a position of greater power than any I've held since. I was a quite efficient disciplinary bureaucrat, operating with the arrogance the job traditionally demanded and with an added quiet menace generated by my understandably distant attitude to the whole thing. It was splendid cover. On one occasion I even evaded a compulsory mass chest X-ray call by marshalling the entire school, boys and masters, onto the buses that took them to the radiography centre, then omitting to join the trip myself.

I didn't get the Cambridge scholarship. My motivation was too oblique, and my preparation hopelessly inadequate; the school wasn't equipped for such work. I had to fall back on Birmingham and its medical, and make the most of the months that remained. When I left school my remote and disaffected manner earned me a beta-plus for Personality in place of the

40

customary straight A awarded to Head Prefects. It was an unprecedented snub. I thought it no bad score, for a corpse.

Going to the university changed my spectral life hardly at all. I cycled a couple of miles beyond the school each day, to the old Arts Faculty building in the city centre. I didn't know at first what course my school had enrolled me for. It didn't matter. I didn't buy books; I made notes in the backs of old school exercise books. I got caught up in a student jazz band, and decided to stay alive until its November Carnival gig; my medical would probably not fall due till February or March.

But the call came early. I cycled halfway to the medical centre, hallucinated chest pains, and phoned in my excuses. I was told to see my own doctor. He told me I had flu, completely failing to observe the wrecked condition of my lungs. Nobody at the postponed medical spotted anything either. The chest X-ray I had would show it all, though. Waiting for the recall, I heard of other students being called in for repeats. But no message came for me. My game was up and I had to recognise it. I was alive, and must immediately adjust to the fact. Instantly and completely, I forgot the delusion which had dominated my life for three years. I mentioned it to nobody, and didn't remember it for a further two years. It was only then that I understood how mad I'd been, and it was the forgetting I found more frightening than the delusion itself.

After that moment in my nineteenth year, I had to begin my life, at the point to which my long absence had let it drift. I had to learn—and quickly— to study, smoke, drink, dance, compete, talk to girls, get around generally. At first I worked frantically to catch up lost ground, with the simple aim of not getting thrown out of the university. I overshot and did rather well, made friends, got around. The local jazz scene of which I'd been a part for a year or two was in a trough, and there was less in it for me. While I was still at death's door I'd played solo at a big concert (insisting, in the interests of secrecy, that my name be excluded from all publicity) and had been invited to make a record for review in the leading jazz magazine—which I did. But the game was turning sour; maybe I realised that in my years away I'd equipped myself, technically, only very poorly and wasn't going to be able to sustain the chances that were coming my way. I broke engagements abruptly, and gave up playing in public for quite a few years.

I came to feel, as I turned nineteen, that I ought to want to write. I seemed to be becoming the sort of young man who had that wish. Thomas

Mann's *Doktor Faustus*, which I first read about this time, had a good deal to do with it; my recent experience qualified me to be sceptical about its thesis, but the account of Leverkühn's artistic education made deliberate creative work seem possible. The insights linked up with something that had happened three years before, at the very onset of my imaginary malady, but which had had to remain isolated and dormant. The school sent a party of us to a belated piece of wartime cultural education. For the time it was something unheard of: a three-day course in film education. Fine gentlemen—Charles Frend, Michael Balcon, Roger Manvell—lectured us about their close experience of this art, and had us sitting goggling at films the like of which we'd never seen before: *Metropolis, Alexander Nevsky, The Plow That Broke the Plains, Night Mail, Steel, Drifters*. There was nothing academic about it all. It just hit hard. Again, there was a disruptive sense of what was possible. I don't think it strange that *Doktor Faustus* didn't make me want to be a composer, just as the film course didn't make me want to direct films; I've grown used to having poetic ideas opened up by arts other than poetry.

Gradually, I got the idea of writing into focus, chiefly by reading, wave on wave of whatever contemporary or recent work I could get hold of, altering taste and orientation by the week. In September 1949, I began keeping an intense, precious journal of my sensibility, and within a month had arrived at a poem. It was meant as a pledge of allegiance to early Dylan Thomas, and every word of it was false, but to be able to write it at all gave me a sense of exultant power. Naturally, I kept the whole thing to myself. I wrote more: pastiches of Auden, Empson, Henry Reed, in rapid succession. Writing was very difficult. I had a certain ability at phrase-making, but no facility of thought or form at all. I was working against resistances quite as formidable as the manual and theoretical problems posed by the piano keyboard.

After nearly a year, my reading had taken me to a stage where I could understand poetry as going beyond verbal sensations to a way of analysing cultures, and I wrote, in some excitement and with much more assurance, a short dramatic monologue in pentameters. The speaker was a King Lear analogue, and he spoke severally through the mouths of Yeats, Rilke, Eliot, and Rafael Alberti—and probably more. There were a few poets around the university: R. F. Willetts was teaching Greek, D. J. Enright was an extramural tutor, and Paul West, not yet a novelist, was a final-year undergraduate. They often attended a staff-student writers' group. I read my piece there, and got plenty of encouragement. The university magazine published it; a door of sorts was opening.

I graduated, well enough to be given a research scholarship, and proceeded to go quietly to pieces again. I'd been good at quick, impressionistic criticism, but didn't know how to work systematically. I was setting out to solve some of the conundrums of metrical analysis, but was too full of a sort of libertarian dogmatism to get anywhere with it. I'd been running with a pack of Jungians and reading Robert Graves; my mind was animated but hardly open. I was obsessed with patterns and hierarchies. My poems became flat, dogmatic arrangements of symbols; my imagination was a pan-historic costume drama.

In an act which seems to me far more bizarre than my imaginary illness, but of which I'm more ashamed, since it was real, I joined a Christian church, on an intellectual whim. I decided that the cult of the Great Mother was magically perpetuated in the sacraments of the Christian church, and that I needed to receive those sacraments in order to share that magical linkage. The ultimate aim would be to subvert the Christian churches back into the Old Religion. I positioned myself at the highest, most ritualistic point of Anglo-Catholicism I could find, took the sacraments, and acquired a pious religiosity, while keeping my real intentions from my instructors. All this was most perverse, for I've always had a deep repugnance for Christianity, in its essence, and for its role in history—an attitude similar to that of Edward Gibbon, and held for similar reasons. But unaccustomed to action or commitment, I was forcing myself against my own nature—was, in fact, forcing my nature to abdicate and submit to something alien and uncongenial.

This went on for a year or two, fading slowly. It wasn't a good period. My scholarship wasn't renewed, for my intellect was being seriously disabled by its own efforts, and by my naïve flailing around for something—preferably something stuffy—to believe in. I'd edited the university magazine, but had run out of steam early and relinquished the editorship. I was still living with my parents, but was withdrawn into my own preoccupations, and oppressed by their many troubles; I was drawn to try to help them, but felt powerless. They were now in their sixties and seeming older. My father's health was breaking down by way of a series of strokes; he was often very anxious, and the damage to his brain brought his thinking and talk down into a more and more limited compass.

In my last year at the university I tried to continue my research while training as a teacher. It wasn't a career I wanted to follow, but I had no other plans, and it was the only job I'd ever watched anyone else doing extensively. Occasionally I wrote doctrinaire fantasy poems, but published only a few of them, I socialised a good deal; my friend Barbara Venables and I spent most of our time at the theatre or in pubs, dressing up and laying the law down. We got married while we were still both students. We were married for many years, and had two sons, Joe and Ben; we stayed friends through that, and remain so now.

My working life started in a characteristically ghostly fashion. When my student exemption from military service ran out, a couple of minor disabilities caused me to be declared unfit, but only on a temporary basis; I could be called in again at any time. The medical exemption was acceptable, for it saved me the trouble of going through the charade of disguising my political objections to military service as reservations of a more tender sort, and still paying a social penalty; but its temporary nature left me in a limbo of an all-too-familiar kind. I could only take a job under false pretences. Which I proceeded to do. I became a teacher at a grammar school in Newton Abbot, in Devon, expecting to be called away at any time, and for that reason living from day to day and putting down no roots. There was no way I could resolve my situation, and instead I treated it as unreal, even to the extent of concealing my address from the authorities and ignoring official summonses when they reached me. Again it was a life of temporary experiences, temporary sensations. It was over a year before an inescapable call caught up with me. This time I failed the medical conclusively. Once again I had to accept my situation as real, and catch up with it.

We lived in Torquay at first, in a squalid, rickety flat, and later in more comfort in Newton Abbot, and I found the area fascinating—for its towns more than its countryside: I'd never lived away from Birmingham before. I'd had no wish to become a schoolteacher; and it was perhaps this lack of seriousness and method which made me turn out to be, from my point of view, disconcertingly good at it. I hated schools as institutions as much as I had done as a pupil, so I treated it all as a compulsory game, and took risks I wouldn't have taken as a serious professional. I read Homer Lane and A. S. Neill, and taught accordingly. The results, of course, were pretty good. Although I didn't enjoy being a teacher, this experience, over the four years I spent there, taught me more about living in the real world than did all my explorations of the West Country. Those gave me enormous pleasure, but they contributed only to my increasingly tortuous fantasy life, which started, in about 1954, to break out into poems again. It was about that time that I came across the work of John Cowper Powys; different from me in almost every imaginable way, he was nevertheless able to show me how to accept an obsessional, quite unpresentable inner existence, a private madness, as a life force to be harnessed rather than locked in and ignored. For a while I worked more in the hope of producing massive novels like his than of making poems. Such poems as I did write were bulky and suffused, or manic, completely dedicated to psychic self-exploration. I'd grown out of the cold ritualism of a few years before, but there was nothing in my poems that might interest anybody else, except a certain energy and a perverse rhetorical force.

It was that odd energy which got me into publication and into touch with what has turned out to be my work. In 1954 a couple of my shorter fantasy poems were broadcast in a local radio programme run by Charles Causley, and some time later John Sankey took one for his nonconformist little magazine, *The Window*. I thought nothing of this, I'd been paid seven-and-sixpence, on condition that I let Sankey alter one line, and had grown out of the poem anyway; but I was surprised to receive a letter from one of the other contributors, Gael Turnbull, whose (as it seemed to me then) perilously slight, purist lyrics I'd noticed. He'd been commissioned to furnish a selection of new British poetry for an issue of Cid Corman's *Origin*, then still in its first series, and, importantly, close to the most vital initiatives in the poetry of Black Mountain College. The mandate was to find British poets who were outside the orthodoxy of the time. I was no Black Mountain poet; I was just another muffled English provincial eccentric. But I was certainly well outside the neat, socially-oriented orthodox poetic, which had neither appeal nor meaning for me. I couldn't even mimic it.

Gael Turnbull, part Scot, part Swede, educated in England and the United States, and just returned from a spell in Canada to work in a London hospital before settling in Worcester, was another inevitable outsider; we had that much in common. Apart from the entrée to *Origin*—Corman approved of what I was doing and used three of my more lightly constructed fantasy pieces—he was able to show me a great deal. On a two-day visit to Worcester late in 1956, I saw for the first time the work of the later Williams, Basil Bunting, Robert Duncan, Alan Ginsberg, Louis Zukofsky, Irving Layton, Robert Creeley, Lawrence Ferlinghetti, Denise Levertov, Charles Tomlinson, Larry Eigner, and Charles Olson. I'd never seen poetry used as these people were, in their various ways, using it, nor had I seen it treated as so vital an activity. These people were behaving with all the freedom and artistic optimism of painters. Decidedly un-English.

I went home and tackled my writing from a new direction. I had already on occasion used chance operations to begin poems I didn't think important; now I used such methods extensively—usually short phrases picked at random, often by my wife, Barbara, who would sometimes arrive at them by automatic writing. The main effect of the method was to get me out of my own way. This was very necessary. I'd grown up with no trace of the compact self which most other people seemed to have; instead I had a diffused zone in which *ad hoc* selves would be generated for temporary purposes, and then dissolve again. Establishing a usable, consistent self was later to prove a lengthy business, like growing a windbreak. The self I'd tried in those days to fix as a writing persona was just a kind of self-important bruise, a posture. It got in the way, and didn't ring true. Once rid of it, though, I could get at observations, memories, earlier selves, lost feelings, casual things—reality, in short—and my clotted language cleared like a cloudy liquid left to settle. Almost immediately a poem called 'Midlanders' turned up; it didn't quite succeed, but it showed me for the first time that I had material close to hand, from my own experience, and access to an unforced way of handling it. Although by my earlier standards my new poems were oblique, casual, and obscure, people started reading them and publishing them. Before long I was in receipt of postal tutorials from Cid Corman and correspondence from Denise Levertov, Larry Eigner, and the British poets and editors Robert Cooper and Bill Price Turner. I was out when Louis and Celia Zukofsky called at our flat in Newton Abbot; but they called, nevertheless.

Gael Turnbull was, in the years that followed, single-handedly responsible for whatever currency I had as a poet. I'd send bundles of work off to him as I wrote it. He was in touch with many editors, and would quietly place my work in magazines I'd not even heard of. I seldom tried pushing my work even then, having a gift for choosing the wrong ones. Soon I gave up, and left nature to take its course; for twenty or thirty years I've been able to rely on invitations—partly since I write relatively little.

I was in a liberated mood, too, because I had, or thought I had, the prospect of giving up full-time teaching. I was being given advancement at the school, and that made me uncomfortable, for I was thereby losing my position as a licensed young experimenter and being brought into the hierarchy. In a year or two I'd be in charge of a department, then in line for a headship, which would involve my identifying myself, to a greater extent than I was willing to do, with the generally Christian and conservative ethos of schools of that sort—indeed, most schools. We decided to go back to Birmingham. Barbara would teach—in Devon I'd had the only job for which we were both qualified—while I'd work part-time in a primary school, and, for the rest, build up a connection as a piano player. As it turned out, her teaching job turned into our son Joe, and I had to hang on to a full-time post in a school so hellishly unruly that I resigned before my year was out, with no job to go to.

Luck, and my teaching testimonials, landed me comfortably on my feet in a college of education, in one of the Black Country towns on the western edge of Birmingham. The place was run on breathtakingly hypocritical and paternalist lines, and my political education was considerably advanced; what I learned, I endeavoured to pass on to my students. But the duties were pleasant, and I was more effective as a teacher of teachers than of children directly. The pay was poor, though, and the penury I'd experienced ever since I went onto a payroll was deepening with a family to keep, so I needed all the piano-playing work I could get. We lived for the next thirteen years back in Handsworth, in a house we couldn't at first afford, a few hundred yards from my mother's old home, Ivy Cottage, by then embedded in a housing estate. For the first five of those years I was constantly out at nights, playing in Dixieland bands, bebop quartets, and Black Country dance bands; for a while I was the token white in the Andy Hamilton Caribbean Combo. I played in jazz clubs, town halls, village halls, strip clubs, dance halls, drinking clubs, and hotels. There was still plenty wrong with my playing, but I got by, and enjoyed it. It was a belated version of my surrendered adolescence.

Living in constant, and apparently inescapable debt darkened my spirits to some extent, and I wrote poetry less freely. But I found that returning to Birmingham after an absence had given me an artist's distance from it. I wanted to write about it, and became immersed in its associative power. My journeys through it in connection with my educational work and my piano playing were in all directions at all hours of the day and night. I saw it from the oddest of angles. Without any particular aim I started on the voluminous series of prose pieces and poems which I was to help Michael Shayer to edit down to the Migrant pamphlet *City* which appeared, as my first collection, in 1961.

BRUM BORN

Until I was thirteen years old and went an hour or so's bus ride to Malvern for my first holiday, I slept every night of my life within the city limits, mostly in the house I was born in. I can think of three nights away in all that time, one in the local hospital, two with relatives a couple of miles away; there were days out in the country but it was always a Birmingham darkness we came back to sleep under. It was a thorough-going preparation for a static life, and I've never become anything of a traveller. It seems an eccentric childhood, but there must have been many like it; and to talk of it only in terms of childhood is a mistake, for my parents shared it all, and many of the people around us lived in the same way. To stay still was quite an appropriate reaction to the place as it was then. It was ugly, but not edgy.

The ugliness was acknowledged. I never then encountered any local patriotism, social or aesthetic. The unspoken view was that the city was a single unalterable circumstance, the major fact of life, not susceptible of questioning. It lay across a fairly gentle landscape, almost devoid of vantage points and vistas, and was a physical thing, a continuous integument of slate and red brick. I can remember going out on to the roof of the highest building in the city centre that had an all-round view, expecting a clear insight into what I knew as a maze of street-level detail but on a hot afternoon the entire place was a reddish-brown saucer, its surface impacted and dull.

I would sometimes play a game of trying to measure its thickness—the height of its buildings—against its extent, about nine or ten miles in each direction. The result was a ratio of something like 1:1000, and the thing was in fact a very thin lacy mineral membrane laid across the land, flimsy and brittle, yet able to occlude the old alignments of open country and dictate new ones of its own. If you were in it, you knew you were. You made yourself at home if you could.

Nowadays the same city is less a place than a continuous construction and transportation event, a perpetual set of traffic and parking problems. For twenty years it has been desperately rebuilt and re-routed. It looks, sounds and feels worse and worse, but getting about in it is far easier, as is getting out. So it seems smaller. And the dominant parts of the new, applied system, the motorways and the tower block estates, genuinely dominate your sense of the place as nothing in the old city did. Then the chief effects were of immovable substances and measureless distance, street on street, suburb on suburb. The centre had always been cramped and improvised, with a few small dignities and no more than three main streets; many people never went there at all, but did everything they had to do within a limited few square miles of the nondescript outer-city-stuff that stretched all round it.

If I look in myself for anything that might be called nostalgia for things gone, what I find is anything but the usual parade of well-loved, fondly remembered public focal points, particular pubs, theatres, cafes and customs, that could add up to a vanished way of social life. When I was a student and a denizen of the city centre I lived on a circuit of places of that kind—Mason College, Yates's Wine Lodge, the Mecca Casino, the Reference Library, the Troc., the Kardomah, and an extraordinary café called Nick's, which had an atmosphere like the bottom of a drain—but only for a while. My real recollections are of private and aimless impressions, glimpses down strange streets, blistering sunlight on giant bridge girders, the smell of coalyards—idylls and hells made out of the only materials to hand. Most of all I remember the conviction that always, just over the next built-up skyline but one, there were unseen worlds, romantic because unseen but inevitably made of just the same constituents as the small patch I knew.

These were not evaluations that passed with childhood. They lasted through adolescence and a few years of absence, and were still accessible when I returned to Birmingham in the late 1950s. The reconstructions were then just starting, late and slow. Demolitions and excavations looked casual and piecemeal though on an epic scale. For a while they seemed to express and add to the older city, while in reality they were signalling its end. All the options still seemed open. In those days I was living in the city on an odd life-rhythm. As a part-time jazz-club musician I was often going to work just as almost everybody else went home; I would be hanging about at times when others were purposeful; I would be crossing town after midnight; if I slept badly I would be taking aimless bus journeys at six in the morning and walking remote suburbs where I knew nobody. All this intensified my habit of looking obliquely at things, thinking thoughts about them which were no part of the original design, and it generated the prose-and-poetry sequence 'City', which is essentially of that period. Earlier, the impressions would have had no urgency; later they could not have existed. By the mid 1960s, when my work involved my travelling all over the city by car briskly, day after day, it was clear that the entire place was on the move along with me. Streets filled day and night with fast traffic are never seen as objects, motionless totems; streets full of parked cars change their nature and the architecture is downgraded, even if it was mean to start with.

The view of the city I grew up with was, on reflection, surprisingly architectural on a modest level, a matter of building materials thrown together into very odd everyday shapes. Garden walls, houses with faces, pavements of blue Rowley Rag bricks stamped with Maltese crosses. If I walk now through Handsworth, my home district, I can see how these familiar hard-working constructions are subjected to an increasing barrage of vibrations, grit, footsteps, fumes, and physical marks of all the pressures of the life that goes on there. Of that life I have said nothing here, and I know I have described a city of which I appear to have been the sole inhabitant, a strange man-made travesty of a Wordsworthian upland. There have been times and moods when that is exactly how it has been for me, and I have always assumed it to be so in part for everybody who experiences it.

Talks for Words

1

I'm improvising this talk into a cheap cassette recorder. Or rather, I was. By the time you hear it I shall have transcribed and typed it: the typescript will have been retyped by the BBC and I shall have read it back into a more sophisticated recording machine. Indeed, that's what I'm doing now. But also what I'm doing now is possibly something which won't be caught on the tape at all: I may be switching on my car radio to hear my own voice coming up past my knees, and talking about doing so as it does so.

But now I'm sitting at home a couple of weeks ago, talking into my cassette recorder, and thinking of this moment, a week or so ahead, when I'm reading what I'm saying into another recorder; and this moment a week or so more ahead, when you're listening—and maybe I am too.

There's a certain sacrilege in talking like this. It's not so long since a recorded programme was thought of as somehow ersatz, and I'm certainly not asking you to consider the complex business of reproducing sounds in any technical sense. But I do find it remarkable that to store and transmit words as trivial as these with even so small a degree of sophistication sets the little bits of material I'm using into a variety of different time scales, like dropping corks into a river with varying currents, so that the nows that I'm talking about—and of course as I talk at this minute there are three or four of them present, in my mind—are moving through my ordinary empirical sense of time at different rates, and with different physical surroundings; and yet the ostensible text is one and the same.

To have these not very important bits of material floating through your life over a period of two or three weeks on these different time scales, going into and coming out of these different boxes, is rather strange, and it reminds me of a day years ago when the looseness of the fit between ideas and texts was brought home to me strongly. I'd just been put in charge of a large class of not very able ten- and eleven-year-olds, and one of the first things I asked them to do was write a story. At the end we had a session in which some of them read their work out. One boy at the back was frantic to let us hear what he had done. He jumped up and read, running his forefinger along the lines, something that went like this: "It was totally dark in the cave as we entered. Bradly paid out the rope, taking care not to snag it on the projecting spurs of rock; and as we took our last look at the daylight we all wondered how long it would be before any of us saw it again. We advanced down the damp glistening floor of the tunnel. I could see our leader's light bobbing ahead in the gloom…" and so on. This was a good deal better than I'd been led to expect, and I went over to look at his book. As I approached him he went rather pink, and made a lot of busy movements. The page had nothing but a brief jumble of incoherent marks—and, indeed, he was virtually illiterate. But the limitations of script weren't getting between him and his concentration on his brilliant piece of bluff.

There was another boy, rather slower, less ingenious who was also illiterate; but in his case it was preposterous to use that word, because the one thing he *could* do was form letters beautifully, but without knowing what they meant. He'd learned a very careful and elegant italic hand, in which he could write his own name, and any combination of letters that gave him manual and visual pleasure in writing.

He was less eager to read, because he knew that what his hand had written wasn't a guide to the words he'd thought, and he had less gift for extemporising. But when I looked at his page, it was a beautiful piece of lettering, clean and even. His favourite letter combinations were those containing a gh; and if you read his piece aloud it would go: "EGHECHI – EGHEGH – ECEOGHI – EGHIGIII – ONCEGH." He couldn't, of course, read back the sounds I've just made; but being literate, I can. Indeed, I've no alternative.

Now, as I said when I started, at some stage in the transmission of these ideas to you from my original tape, I shall have transcribed them, and the typist will have retyped then very clearly for me to read. But at this moment there's something only the producer, the typist and I know. And that's whether the script I'm reading from is one in which I let the typist do the whole script using only her own favourite five letters on the keyboard; or whether it's one in which I insisted she confine herself to my favourite three.

2

Alex Comfort, in *Sex and Society*, coined the intriguing phrase "adulterous prop". This simply describes the function of those long-suffering, or short-suffering, individuals who help to keep somebody else's marriage going by diverting one of the partners from his or her boredom or misery. Years ago I watched a *Man Alive* feature about a brisk and jolly lady whose chosen role was to be, over and over again, just such a prop—the perpetual Other Woman. She obviously plied her hobby with deftness and style, but one thing she said was chilling. It went something like this. "And just when they're feeling satisfied and mumbling nice things with their eyes shut, I lean over them on the pillow, and make them look at me. *What is my name?* I say, *What's my name?*" She particularly enjoyed it when they got it wrong. This was shown at the time when you couldn't help being reminded of the voice of Muhammad Ali, slamming Ernie Terrell round the ring to the sound of those same words, when Terrell had taunted him under his discarded name of Cassius Clay.

It must be a fine thing to have some stability in your name, some sense that it identifies you, even if you've had to alter it to reach a satisfying effect. When I was a boy I was relieved for a time to have escaped being called Walter, after my father, or Barnabas, after the saint whose day I was born on; but later I might have been glad to have had either in place of the weak flavourless monosyllable I was given. In the accents of my native town it had a little character, in that it came out as *Rye*; but when people started getting it right it seemed a complete cipher, hard to live down to.

In fact, it was many years before I really had to accept it. I lived first through a series of applied names, all of which seemed appropriate at the time: The Bab; Fatty; Podgy; Fish. When I was quite small strangers would look at me and say "Howdo, George!" and I thought there must be some truth in that, if I looked like a George even at first sight. And most people who knew perfectly well who I was would call me by the name of my quite different older brother. I suppose that while I was making instantaneous translations of what made sense to them into what made sense to me I was learning to expect a profound discontinuity between names and things.

Later, when I was a schoolmaster I once had an experience which made me feel I was hearing my most real name. I was approaching a rowdy classroom. The lookout boy saw me coming, rushed into the room, and

I heard him cry "Ssh! Here comes—" and he said a name. I didn't hear it perfectly; it sounded like *Snafty* or *Slafty*. I'd never heard it before, and I didn't bother to ask what it had been, because I knew I wouldn't get a true reply, but I felt I'd heard the name I was really known by—and there's no name more binding than a teacher's nickname. I did, however, as a teacher, have a name I was happier with than with most of my names. I was Sir, just used as a proper noun, not as a title. "I'll tell Sir!" In my mind I spelled it like a French reflexive, *se*—s.e. It seemed the proudest, freest, most self-regarding name you could have.

After the ontological insecurity brought on by my own unstable naming, the naming of both my sons was carried out on the principle of combining certitude with flexibility. Each was given a first name suitable for a life of rough and ready likeability; a second name suited to a career of relentless social climbing; and a third to be used in the event of advanced narcissistic decadence. Both boys took immediately to their first names and stuck to them, and probably will do so even if their lives came to belie the labels.

For my part, I live now openly under my given names, but in a place called Larchwood, which is not a larch wood, but a large grassy square with a few deodars at one end, to lend conviction.

3

Saul Steinberg once made a famous series of drawings of people's speech, in which a succession of talking heads emitted visual equivalents of their speech characteristics—from one, a cloud of birds; from another, a bouquet of flowers, from another, an ornate building; from another, tangles of what looked like horsehair—and you knew, without a single word being referred to, just what language personality each of these people had. The heads were characterised so that you could see how appropriate what came out of each mouth was; and indeed the patterns were expressions of personality—personal offerings. They needn't have been anything to do with speech at all; they could have been designs for personalised wallpaper or dress fabrics. But the fact that Steinberg chose to link then to the act of speaking brings out two points that are interesting. One is that by making a *graphic* description of language he's by-passing the almost inevitable air of pedantry which comes over anybody who sits down to *talk* solemnly about anything so mercurial as language; and the other is that his firm linking of language to individuality seems to assume that some of us at least live in quite personal worlds of language. It's as if the people in the drawings had borrowed, or leased, the makings of their language from a common stock, but had used that stock—what we usually call "the language"—merely as a basis for rich personal variations, much as people buy mass-produced cars and immediately set to to redesign them out of all recognition.

Steinberg's being a caricaturist and not a linguist; and he's not propounding a general rule. The drawings I've mentioned do put an exaggerated stress on idiosyncrasy. If you put the horsehair, the birds, the blossoms, the buildings together and didn't say what they represented, they wouldn't have much in common.

In reality, of course, the idiosyncratic elements in anybody's speech or writing constitute only a minute proportion of it, but it acts like a drop of concentrated flavouring, dispersing itself through the whole. And we're able to respond to it very sensitively, just as we respond to the extremely complex information-sorting which we do when we recognise somebody's face, and know it from all other faces. I can think now of the talk of people I've not heard for many years, some of them long since dead, and with their voices unrecorded. But to say *what* I think, *how* I'm able to remember them, is very difficult. I can only put it in some such way as this—I can say, for example, "I can imagine my grandfather talking." I certainly don't get an auditory hallucination, that is, I don't hear a voice; I don't even get a sense that distinguishable words or messages are being uttered. But I do have, still ready for use, though it's been in storage since his death more than thirty years ago, a configuration of disembodied tones, inflections, turns of phrase—the recognition-kit for that individual language that was my grandfather's. And I suppose that although I shall never need to use it again in its own right, since I shall never hear its owner again, I'm still referring to it from time to time as part of my general orientation towards new voices I'm learning.

A biologist would make his own sort of comment on this hypertrophy of our ability to distinguish among other individuals of our own species on a minutely detailed level; what interests me is how we use it socially. We're all familiar with self-appointed word-watchers who position themselves along the sea wall ready to raise the flood alarm if they hear a single syllable slip; and many of us have had the uncomfortable experience of finding we think less well of a friend who makes a spelling mistake, even though we know the spelling rule's both illogical and ridiculously demanding. It's easy to be over-sensitised to the signals.

I can say this even though I come from Birmingham, a place which is popularly supposed to be the home of the utmost linguistic crudity; a place whose inhabitants are believed to have brass throats, gaping mouths full of grit, and cloth ears since if they could hear themselves they wouldn't speak the way they do. The local accent's one nobody ever wants to acquire; even actors and comedians hardly ever listen to it for long enough to learn more than its simplest features. In fact, though, in terms of the subtleties of English pronunciation and usage, it's a region of perpetual muffled fighting, a borderland between the embattled North and the complacent South. Or rather, since the military metaphor has too much of commitment about it, it's a human market place where market forces rule; where successive generations of the same family will have different accents; where members of the same household will choose their accents and maintain them or modify then without attracting any great attention to themselves thereby; where individuals will go beyond the ordinary bilingualism of work-speech and home-speech and take their language up-market and down-market again over different periods of their lives. The local language is fluid: its variations reflect personal status, aspiration or resignation more than any minor regional origins. I think it's more rarely than in other industrial cities that you'll find examples of the old language still showing through, archaic, against the tide: the little boy, left on his own on a playing field, crying miserably: "Ah wor puk!" That is to say, "I wasn't picked!" Unless he learns the language of the main chance, he won't be.

5

Anybody who's ever been tongue-tied will know the enormous force of one's own silence. I'm not talking about extreme cases, like drying up on stage, with everybody waiting to hear your next word, when you can't even remember what a word *is*: I'm talking about silences which can be quite prolonged without attracting much attention at all. I teach for a living, which means that for a large part of the time I talk too much, having learned some sort of fluency by necessity. And sometimes in a group discussion I have to check myself and reflect that somebody who has volunteered nothing, yet isn't obviously asleep or writing a letter, may well be undergoing an experience I've often had. This consists of following the conversation of several other people, quite actively, but at a slight remove in time, so that the conversation always slightly outpaces you, as if it were being relayed by satellite. You never lose touch with it, but the little time-lags you need for finding words are being withheld, or obstructed by somebody else who jumps in with something that takes the subject away from where you were. And unless you make an issue of wanting to speak, by calling a halt, or unless somebody does the same by calling directly on you to find your tongue, it's possible to spend an hour or two in company—some people obviously spend virtually their whole lives like this— with unspoken thoughts, half-verbalised; uncontributed contributions; and if they haven't spoken, then on a *conversational* scorecard they have scored zero, even though they have a considerable build-up of near-conversation. These words may be left swilling around in the head; and that brings with it very often the familiar sense of the language discharged later to oneself, the conversation—both sides of it—which never developed; the conversation there might have been.

This is a rebound-language which isn't being used, except for clarification, and these dead and frustrated bits of conversation are converted to one of the other uses of language, which is the language of introspection. I suppose anybody will use that language when devising something important; but of course some people must live very large parts of their mental lives, their linguistic lives, on this strange relayed level of crypto-conversation, I can remember times when language of that sort, rattling away in the head, jabbering away in my own ear, could blot out what I felt was the proper business of my mind. It would get between me and the world. The only virtue the experience had was to make me feel at least capable of sympathy for the plight of the policeman who comes to my door with a solemn, open, confidence-inspiring manner and maybe a serious message; but his message, to say nothing of his manner, always gets cut into by a strange strangulated parrot voice that suddenly comes squawking out of his chest from the radio-phone. He's learned to ignore it, but I can't.

There's one example of an interior, or internalised language which has always fascinated me, though I've never found it attractive. George Orwell would, for practice, verbalise any experience he had time to verbalise; that is, he would write it in his head as it was happening, would convert it into a realistic narrative; so that on entering a room he would 'render' it, like an artist sketching; he would imagine how it would need to read. I've never really wanted to try this: the verbal rendering of a scene is bound to be affected by the characterisation of whoever's looking at it. Orwell's eye and language would be different from Alain Robbe-Grillet's. I'd be wary of inwardly talking myself into the character of a know-all reporter who can find words for just about anything.

I started by talking about silence, the social silence of failing to start talking. Possibly a great deal of that failure can be blamed on our excessive respect for the delicate conventions of entering conversations. Not everybody conforms. I'll give just two examples of originality. Once I travelled a long way on a rainy night to hear a reading by a visiting American poet for whose work I had, and have, a great respect. Ushered into a hall of complete strangers, he had the demeanour of a man who was ready to start by saying how glad he was to be there, and so forth. The chairman welcomed him and withdrew, leaving him to introduce his reading. So far as my recollection goes, his first words were: "Notwithstanding, at all events, the significance of the attention as placed, towards with quote regard unquote location…" We were soon off in pursuit, but some felt winded from the start. The other example comes from the early career of a young man I know. He first showed he wasn't like everybody else at the age of about three, when he walked into a room full of people, looked penetratingly at the company, said, very clearly, "Besides which!" and left. Besides which—

6

Long ago I formed the idea of becoming a poet by writing poems. I'd tried painting, and I'd tried music, but had been oppressed by the difficulty of avoiding academic training in these arts—an avoidance which at the time seemed to me essential. But it was a time when nobody in this country would have suggested that it was possible or desirable to teach imaginative writing beyond the rudiments of school composition, so my way was clear. My readings about poetry threw up very few prescriptions, and I was sorry rather than glad to find even those. I can remember struggling, rather unwillingly, to take to heart the warnings Wystan Auden issued in the preface of his selection from Tennyson. He said that if a young man came to him full of important things he wanted to say, then that young man would never be a poet; if, on the other hand, he said "I like hanging around words, listening to what they say," then maybe one day he would be a poet. I thought this a piece of rather mystical pedantry, but I saw the force of it. And it was probably my first acquaintance with the anthropomorphic view of language, the suggestion that it has a will of its own. It's one of those jokes that feeds off a real unease.

At any rate, I set about writing my poems, and kept at it. It was probably my own fault that the first twenty years weren't much fun; at any rate there was a moment after the first ten when dissatisfaction got the better of me and I dashed off a piece of self-mocking doggerel, in which the art of poetry figured as an insatiable nuisance, a hole in the floorboards into which I stuffed anything I could find, worthless or valuable, in an effort to stop the draught and get some peace. It ended like this:

I prodded lengths of string
down with a long pin,
I fetched water and milk,
and let them trickle in;
lead shot, nail-parings, currants,
torn-up paper bags,
splinters that once were furniture
my clothes cut into rags;
and so, morsel by morsel,
till its last trick was sprung,
I poked my life away into
the bland English tongue.

The mood that produced that piece has long since left me; but I can recreate quite easily the particular pleasure it gave me in the final line to turn and bite my own language—*the bland English tongue*. And that was the real target for my recriminations—not poetry itself, which still seemed a world of fine possibilities, but the language I had to write in, which I thought pallid and limp in its sounds and its structures. I'd been caught, of course, in the trap Auden had described. I'd been trying to make poems out of huge, fateful ideas, and had been greedily huffing and puffing at the language to make things happen. I had I suppose done my share of hanging around words listening to what they said, in terms of Auden's preferred course of action; but having listened to what they'd said, I'd thought it effete.

I'd been brought up to appreciate the rich resources of English as an expressive language, particularly from Chaucer onwards; to understand the huge range of its metaphoric and rhythmic potential, and the sinuousness of its syntax. On the shadier side I was also intimately familiar with the fiendish intricacies of the nuances of servility and dominance which it contributes to its ignoble alliance with our class-ridden society system. But for me the strength was a sunset glow, and the flexibility was the flexibility of a watch by Salvador Dalí—the sort that drips over the edge of a chest of drawers like a strip of liver.

At any rate, that's how it seemed. I had too little faith, I wasn't ready to listen; and I recant. But I can't help regretting our socially-generated prevalence of deferential or diffident turns of phrase and speech tunes, or the loss from Standard English of some of the strongly-formed consonants the Scots and Northumbrians still have.

You can't play Canute with language. It must change; and if the changes don't match your purpose, then your work is that much the harder. I tend to take plenty of holidays into festive sub-languages just outside the city limits of English. Foreign film subtitles, for instance, with their continual tiny cliff-hangers in mid-sentence. Or the pithy names of German-American jazz musicians—the trumpeter Lyman Vunk, the drummer Kurt Bong, of the Oskar Doldinger Trio; or the early existentialist tuba player who was a member of Owen Fallon's Californians in 1925—one Hartmann Angst.

In the end, language has to be accepted, if with resignation. If I had been without language until this moment, and were offered it, I think I might react as Samuel Beckett is reported to have done when they told him he'd won the Nobel Prize. "It is a disaster," he said; and took the money.

The Morden Tower

The Morden Tower's in a different country from most other places where poetry's read; it's better. I first came to it on a winter Saturday early in l965 or 1966, at the end of what was then—I'd grown up with a quite severe travel-phobia—the longest journey I'd ever taken, the train trip from Birmingham to Newcastle, approaching the Tyne under a high, cold, portentous sky, with stacks of murky sunset cloud towering above the city. Tom Pickard met me, a well-grown youth in yellow boots, with a face under his hair; marvellously friendly, optimistic and embattled, and swearing terribly. At the Pickards' flat in Jesmond, Basil Bunting was sitting by the fire with a mug of tea and a notebook, finishing 'What the Chairman Told Tom', which he'd been writing on the train from Wylam; later, in the sagging throne of an armchair by the smoky fire in the Tower, he gave it its first reading. I was an uneasy reader in those days, and most of the poetry I had to read was such sour stuff it depressed even me; but the palpable receptivity for poetry in that dusty, dimly-lit room leaned back against what I'd brought, and held it up. I've never read at the Tower without learning something.

My Trip to Brighton

I went to Brighton only the once. To do so hadn't occurred to me previously and although the idle thought of going again did appear once or twice over the succeeding years the call never came.

It was in the early summer of 1977. I'd been booked, on whose initiative I forget, to read in an afternoon three-hander with Michael Hamburger and Lee Harwood in the Friends' Meeting House. I left my house at Keele early and drove to Stoke to catch a London train. It was a public holiday for the Queen's Silver Jubilee, I remembered, and there was little traffic, though I was apprehensive at the thought of crossing London on a festive day. The train was half-empty. At Euston late in the morning I dived straight into the underground and didn't set eyes on the streets of London. With only a subdued handful of others I took the tube under the city to Waterloo, sliding quietly a few yards beneath whatever processions, crowds and little flags were at that same hour having their way up top.

Walking the almost-deserted arc of Waterloo to find the Brighton train I suddenly saw a wavy vision in the colours of straw and sky crossing the platform at a fast trot. Joanna Lumley, legging it in stack heels to catch a train out of town, one hand clutching an enormous grab-bag, the other holding an enormous hat secure. I gawped. She grinned back and kept on running. We've not met. The next new experience was to learn where Gatwick Airport was, something I'd never wondered.

Lee met me from the train and we walked to his flat for lunch, then to the Meeting House, where there was an audience, none of whom I knew. I'd expected to see Andrew Crozier, by then a few years at Sussex University after having been my colleague at Keele; but I learned later that he'd assumed the reading, out of respect for Her Majesty, would not be taking place. Lee read, earnestly and lightly; Michael read, earnestly and wistfully. I can remember nothing now of what each of us felt moved to deliver at that time.

Then back to the train and a reverse reprise of my furtive-feeling journey into, through, and beneath the crowded heart of the land, busy with street parties, fireworks and television. Still nobody down in the underground and I was home by late evening ready for work the next day and feeling strangely untouched by the sweat of the capital. Neither do I recall having seen the sea that day in Brighton though it must have been visible from our walk. Not that I've any aversion to the sea. In South

Devon I'd lived within daily sight of it for years and had come to prefer it to the suffused ruddy landscape of those parts. But in Sussex I had no sense of having reached the end of the land, so took no pains to have that confirmed. One of Lee's postcards might do the job.

Six Towns

In the early Nineties I was having little contact with poetry. My collaboration with Tom Pickard on his Arts Council film about Birmingham was completed and I had no project in view other than playing all the gigs I could take on while I still had the use of both my hands, a period that turned out shorter than I'd expected. There was fearful illness in the house, and that pre-empted most of my imagination. I had a jaded relationship with a publisher, which didn't encourage me to work; and all in all the poetry web was not supporting me in any way I could find useful. Not a disappointment: simply an area of my life that seemed ready to repay the neglect I'd often given it.

I didn't find it strange to be contacted by a young man with plans for some new poetic activity. What was surprising was, first, picking up his assumption that I was as enthusiastic and optimistic as he was, and, second, realising the extent and quality of his knowledge of the work and circumstances of a variety of poets driven by curiosity and dedication but almost without exception incapable of having their names lodged in the memories of journalists or even competition judges. I didn't exactly try to dissuade Nicholas [Johnson] from attempting to set up a festival in a location I knew to be unreceptive, but I soon knew, when I saw him with the infant Louis in a pushchair patiently leafletting Buxton, a town 30 miles from the Potteries, that we were already out beyond prudence and economy of effort. I also knew, when I was issued with a rubber stamp reading FESTIVAL PATRON, that I was in some sense on board, if without portfolio.

As the first programme was building, with talk of shared transport and ad hoc accommodation and food, it was a source of some personal pain to me to realise that a new generation of promoters and organisers was arriving with no knowledge that a system of funding readings, originally the initiative of the Association of Little Presses, had ever existed although it had managed its small budget efficiently for years (agreed fees by cheque at the reading, hotels and travel pre-arranged) and was only recently dead, having inadvertently allowed its resources to be dispersed, often falling into the sludge at the bottom of local authority Sport and Leisure budgets where they lacked the critical mass to maintain identity and were wasted. All the same, the absence of these formalities made a party atmosphere compulsory, all the better for the poetry.

The Festival's relation to the Potteries was probably as slight as I'd predicted. Among the readers and their visiting followers there was a strong Scottish presence as well as a significantly unpredictable one from Ireland. The place could easily attract audiences from London, and did so. Time made it clear that the festival gained an identity from its unusual title while remaining essentially nomadic, setting up camp wherever the founder could find pasture for his yak.

Ric Caddel

Ric's mind was settled early and without fuss. I first heard from him when he invited me to give a Colpitts reading soon after he'd started the series, and the undogmatic, uncluttered assurance of his outlook was already apparent.

For a later visit he produced a flyer with a few of my poems. The cover reproduced an antique line drawing of a group of well-grown, complacent-looking onions. Without being told, he'd gone to my favourite and most appropriate vegetable. I asked him where he'd found the illustration. "In a book of onions," he said. And there you had it. He was a man who knew there were books of onions, and that was that.

As an editor and publisher he treated me perfectly. He would propose an available space, somehow get me to feel it would be safe for me to occupy it, and then simply clear off. In this way he was able to generate several pieces of mine which would otherwise never have come about. And on every occasion he did the decent thing and accepted what I sent, whatever my misgivings might have been. He'd been gambling too.

Ric's arrival in poetry by way of music was a prophylactic against literary yapping and snapping; it informed his own writing and was an abiding presence. The last extended conversation I had with him concerned the keyboard eccentricities of Svyatoslav Richter, Glenn Gould and the late Mr Monk. On the previous evening I'd been reading for the Bunting centenary and had been leaned on to play a short slow piece, all I could trick past my partially-paralysed right hand. For this small task, worth a church hall upright at most, he offered me choice of two concert grands: a biddable Steinway and a monster Bösendorfer. "That one," he said, "goes off like an express train once you get it started up." I chose the Bösendorfer. Afterwards, I apologised to Lucy Caddel for the absence of decoration in what I'd done. "Oh, it was good to hear the basics," she said, exercising something stronger than mere tact, and probably hereditary.

Our last encounter of all was, somehow suitably, quite spectral. In the autumn of 2001 I was making daily visits, miles from home, to the hospital in Sheffield where my wife Joyce was having the surgery from which she would eventually fail to recover. Her ward shared an entry corridor with its mirror image opposite. Walking out one afternoon and glancing through, I briefly saw silhouetted against a distant window a figure which would have been Ric's had it not obviously been that of a ward attendant carrying a broom or something similar. Shortly after that I received an email which began: "As I shambled—leaning hard on my stick—into Sheffield Northern General Hospital the other day, I saw a figure—also on stick—moving in the opposite direction, which I thought might be yours, but my mind was woolgathering as usual and by the time I'd surfaced you—or your doppelgänger—had cornered out of view." The Caddels, many more miles from home than I was, were visiting Ann's mother who was lying a few yards from Joyce in what was also to turn out to be a final illness. Ric went on to ask: had I in fact been me? I had to agree it was a possibility.

Spoken at the Funeral of Stuart Mills

Only a few weeks ago Stuart told me he'd been pleased and surprised to hear that I'd publicly described him as "an activist". He had no need to feel surprised, for original initiatives and actions characterised his entire career.

He and I attended, ten years apart, the same Birmingham school: Handsworth Grammar School, a place which unintentionally gave its pupils a solid grounding in scepticism about the traditional values it preached. Then, training as a painter at Birmingham College of Art, Stuart had access to a far more sophisticated view of invention, composition and artistic values than he would have found in a course in English Literature. And when he moved across, as he soon did, into writing, he carried that outlook with him. Already as a young Art teacher, long before his move to Derby College of Art, he was initiating, with one of a succession of gifted collaborators, a series of minority bookshop ventures in Nottingham, the best-known being the Trent Bookshop. These were probably the first of their kind outside London.

From that there quickly developed a programme of poetry readings that culminated in the quite spectacular Nottingham Poetry Festival of 1966; again almost certainly a provincial first for an event on that scale. Along with it came the magazine *Tarasque*, with its press and its poetry pamphlets, developing into Aggie Weston's Editions, an imprint destined to survive in a great variety of forms for well over thirty years. While these activities were developing Stuart also became a tireless traveller, visiting the writers and artists who interested him in their various hideouts and setting up webs of connections and friendships that might otherwise never have been made.

In common with all this, Stuart's own writings, photographs and print designs were dedicated to sharp insights and to pleasure. He always detested anything shoddy, pretentious or fraudulent, and the knowledge that such qualities were flourishing everywhere undoubtedly caused him pain and a sense of battling against the odds. But from the first the spiky judgments were accompanied by an often gleeful delight in sheer mischief. He never attempted to invade the literary mainstream with bulky prestige-seeking works. Instead his poems tended to be brief, elegant, quietly incisive and lightly but very durably constructed; and now that the time has come for them to be collected they will be seen to embody a sustained, lively and sane critique of the art of poetry in his time and beyond it.

License My Roving Hands

I've played jazz on pianos, or the defunct, sodden carcasses of pianos, in hundreds of different establishments since the middle 1940s. But what to call those places? Jazz clubs? Sounds like somewhere specially built, like cocoa rooms or abattoirs; not true. Night clubs? Rarely, and on sufferance. Dance halls? Sometimes. Restaurants? Once in a while. I ought, I sometimes think, to have been pumping out this American-born music all these years in a succession of underground dens, cellars, furnished holes in the sidewalk. *Dives.* But hardly any of them have been that sort of place. Most of them have been up several flights of stairs, and very English indeed. For the overwhelming majority of these venues have been the more-or-less disused Function Rooms of old pubs, with buffalo horns, and bedroomy wallpaper above the brown panelling,

There's a further oddity. In all those years, I can only call to mind a handful of occasions on which I've entered one of those long, dark, linoleum-floored rooms for any purpose other than that of playing or hearing jazz. A small farewell supper for a local headmaster in a Devon market town; a brief sandwich lunch in Cromford, Derbyshire, for our educational coach tour of D. H. Lawrence country; and a couple of working meetings of the Birmingham and district project group of Centre 42. Now those were, as they say, something else. I was there as a jazz musician, but not to play; things hadn't got as far as that. For me they never did.

Arnold Wesker's Centre 42 movement of the early Sixties still has, for me, such a feeling of unfinished business, of unresolved issues, that I find it hard to realise that it all happened, or didn't happen, so long ago that it's bound to need explaining. It was a movement which aimed at raising Trade Union consciousness, and Trade Union funds, in the cause of discovering and fostering real, non-commercial popular culture: art by and for the people. The assumption was that the populace at large had its own arts locked up within it, and, more interestingly, *needed* those arts, and for more vital purposes than mere entertainment; it needed its own arts in order to live as a civilisation, instead of as nothing more than somebody else's army of workers and consumers—for it still seemed fairly natural then, as it would not seem so nowadays, to describe the majority of the population in terms of its work, and even of its membership of unions.

It all sounds uncommonly like—Socialism? Well, yes. That was the idea. A very old idea, of course; a noble old flag-waver of an idea, going back far beyond William Morris and Walt Whitman, and here surfacing once again, however much it had become muddied along the way by new sophistications. Indeed, my own first thought, when the summons to show interest came round in the Musicians' Union newssheet, was that this was all exactly like things I'd read about in accounts of the Left Wing arts movements of the Thirties—Unity Theatre, groups set up by the WPA in America, that sort of thing. But I decided all the same to turn out and see what might be going on. I couldn't imagine that this enterprise wasn't something completely fresh: even if you left the war out of account, and the great tidal movements of national and world politics, there had already occurred the first wave of the Campaign for Nuclear Disarmament, the first wave of Rock music and the first wave of mass television ownership; there had been invasions by foreign films and by the ideas of the Beat Generation; folk clubs were on the up; and there had even been a few changes wrought by bebop and the traditional jazz revival. And for those who live in worlds capable of being changed by such things, the world was about to be changed and out of all recognition and forever by The Beatles and Christine Keeler. So I made my way one evening across yet another pub foyer floored with Victorian mosaic tiles, and up yet another brown staircase, to an upper room, with heavy tables, dark bentwood chairs, and tall windows that overlooked the back of New Street Station.

The gathering wasn't large, nor was it particularly heterogeneous, either; there may have been other stray members of various unions as well as me; I'm not sure. Whatever the details, however, the general makeup of the meeting soon became clear; for it was something I'd seen before, and which I've certainly seen many times since. We were a group of people mostly in what were still in those days thought to be safe middle-class occupations: teachers; an extremely distinguished BBC producer; a hefty presence of Communist Party members from the Public Library Service, the Council House, and also possibly from one or two departments of the University with a long history of that allegiance. And as for me, I was teaching in a College of Education, where the teachers had to be called *lecturers*—a title which had little relation to what most of us actually did, but which seemed to endow the job with an extra coating of protection from misfortune or squalor, even if it didn't enhance our wretched pay.

At a guess, most of the people in the room were in publicly-funded, and probably pensionable, jobs. An old story. But there we were: wherever we'd started out from, individually, we'd got ourselves shunted, by way of education (mostly free), occupational aptitude, and taste, into a sort of siding of middle-class life, from which we were staring out across a social divide that separated us from a *lot* of people. Most people. I'm not suggesting that it was a total separation, or even a dramatic one; we weren't part of a wholly stratified society like that of the Eloi and the Morlocks in Wells's *The Time Machine* where two classes had lived in such separateness that they had eventually evolved into distinct species which might as well never have had a common origin. There were plenty of connections, but they were basic ones. Not all of the finer filaments of the cultural wiring managed to cross the gap, in either direction.

Some of us will have wished the divide had never come into existence; some of us, especially those who, like me, had been involuntarily airlifted across it in our sleep by the educational system, will have wished it had been less marked, so as to allow for free passage to and fro. There might just be a case for the odd Parish Boundary; there was certainly no warrant for the Berlin Wall. At all events, I suppose we were people who were unwilling to be stuck with only the higher forms of art as our only sustenance; and who, moreover, weren't simply in the business of carrying higher culture to the lower orders—or London culture to what London still called "the provinces". We were much more interested in something we suspected might be persuaded to flow in the opposite direction. Our belief—or hope, at the very least—was that there existed, *out there,* or *down there,* valuable knowledge, urgent messages, ways of communicating, which hadn't survived a century or two of erosion and suppression, only to be drowned in recent waves of consumer-pap. We wanted to make contact.

But as soon as that meeting started to get down to a practical programme, I began to experience an inescapable sensation of being gradually squeezed out on to the periphery. And I was never for a moment in any doubt as to which of the people in the room was doing the squeezing: *I* was. There was something going on that wasn't going to work for me, and as the discussion went on I came to feel that I could neither beat it nor join it. This was in spite of the fact that I had— and still retain—a great respect for the work of our strongest asset: the radio producer. This was Charles Parker, a most talented and demanding man, one of the earliest virtuosi of the portable tape-recorder and a pioneer—if you can give that title to somebody whose work wasn't fully followed up—of a form of documentary radio art which worked by letting people speak entirely for themselves, having edited out all traces of the professional broadcaster and interviewer. All traces, that is except the unmissable trace of the hand of the director, who shapes the whole thing; I did say "art". Parker died at sixty, a few years ago, after a period of comparative inactivity and frustration; but at the time I'm speaking of he was in full flight, having quite recently produced, to considerable acclaim, the best examples of the genre he devised, the Radio Ballad. For the Centre 42 project, he was undertaking to oversee a sort of live Radio Ballad, a mixture of documentary material, dramatisation, songs and instrumental music. It was to be a touring show, which would play Labour Clubs, Miners' Institutes and the like, in various manufacturing centres around the Midlands.

It sounded good, and I believe it turned out so, though I never managed to catch it, when it eventually took to the road. There was certainly plenty of talent and experience in the room that night; much of it from the folk-music revival end of things. I suppose that was an element in my self-imposed squeeze-out. Two things were clear: one, that music in the folk-song idiom, genuine or newly-minted, was integral to the production; two, that most of the people present had worked together before and had many assumptions, and a good deal of optimism, in common. I seemed to have dealt myself all the doubts. There wasn't, for instance, any real need for jazz in the production, though there was a willingness to make room for it as a tinge, a coloration, a particular form of expressive energy. The fact that there seemed to be no possible opening for what jazz players, on whatever instrument, sometimes just call *blowing*—letting fly, exercising their faculties at large—wasn't the fault of the project. Had there been other jazz musicians interested, we might have set up an additional project of our own, based on the music; but I was the only one, so I'd have to fit in where I could.

I did try fitting in; but as I listened to the planning, the doubts grew and grew, and they were ideological. Not in terms of straight politics, but in terms of what the potential audience was *like*. I seemed to feel a kind of missionary conviction in the air around me, and as the actual material of the production began to be roughed out, I could see that the Socialist Realism of the thing wasn't going to square with the day-to-day realism of anybody in the bit of the working class I'd come from. For a start, it was all about *work*. And it was going to develop—interestingly enough— into a sort of hymn to the technology of heavy industry. I could see the point of taking the technical wonders of the means of production and drawing them to the attention of those who used those wonderful means but certainly didn't own them; but going straight into the subject seemed to me like jumping the gun. I realised that in the minds of my potential colleagues that gun had been jumped long since. I *was* back in the Thirties after all.

Then came the real wave of doubt. The proposed title went through on the nod. It was 'The Worker and His Tool'. I couldn't believe what I was hearing. I looked furtively around. Not a grin, not a flicker anywhere. Titles for the sections were apportioned: they were things like 'The Shaping of the Tool'; 'The Hardening of the Tool'; 'The Fitting of the Tool' . Memory may exaggerate; but not by much. I didn't dare speak my thoughts. I could envisage the ring of heads turning frozen, uncomprehending stares on me. Who was this sniggering, insecure troublemaker, this slanderer of the seriousness of the worker? So I kept my doubts to myself; with the result that I impressed myself with them, if nobody else. Maybe these people really did know something I didn't? Maybe they'd lived among secret tribes of car workers and blast-furnace operators whose very existence had been hidden from me all my life? If I shut up and did my bit I might learn something new after all.

My bit turned out to be something I simply couldn't deliver, and that was why the second meeting was my last. My assignment had been merely to get hold of a couple more jazz instrumentalists, a double-bass player and a drummer, and get them interested in the project. That has an air of bland possibility about it: why not? I'll tell you why not. Somehow I had to tell the working party why not, but I can't imagine they believed me. I was being asked to create economic havoc. The musicians I was after worked all day in factories, for money. Almost every night of the week they were out playing, for money—and bass players and drummers never came cheap, let alone free. Earning money may just have been a bad habit they'd got into; but I knew from the start that I had no chance of persuading any of them to forgo afternoons and evenings' wages in order to hare off to Atherstone or Wellingborough in pursuit of a cause. I couldn't deliver any bodies. A pity; but there it was.

At that second meeting, though, I wasn't the only spot of teething trouble. A Labour Club in one town couldn't accept the show on the night it could get there, on account of its unshakeable commitment to its own Bingo; in another town the Miners' Club bar, with its fruit machines and juke-box, could on no account be closed during the performance; a genuinely proletarian melodeon player who had been found in a village mostly given over now to executive housing had shown no interest whatever in joining a visit to the city gasworks to meet the workers there and share views. There was a certain impatience in evidence in the upper room that night; it was not far from the situation in that sarcastic poem of Bertolt Brecht's, where he suggests that the government might find things easier if it were to dissolve the people and elect another. It was time for me to fade away from the enterprise, baffled and still surprised at what I'd found; and go back down that particular set of stairs, with never a note struck in anger.

§

Anyone who gets, professionally or semi-professionally, into the business of assembling groups of musicians for dances, clubs or private functions, builds up a very important, and usually rather eccentric, book of telephone numbers. I'm talking only about jazz, or jazz-related music: the sort of thing that relies a good deal on improvisation and on a set of ideas about instrumentation and repertoire, which all the players who are likely to get booked will have in common. They don't even have to share a common language: I once—in Holland, as it happens—had to play a set of trombone-and-piano duets with an Argentinian trombonist. In spite of the fact that some of his musical colleagues had quite recently been sent out, against their wills, by Galtieri and killed, against my will, by British troops, our only problem of communication was finding an interpreter for the words, 'What are we going to play, then?' For it turned out that he knew the English for *Misty* and *Everybody Loves My Baby,* I knew the chords, so we were all set. For both of us, the musical challenge—maybe we met it, maybe we didn't—was the business of working out, as we went along, how to make a reasonable sound out of just a trombone part and just a piano part—a combination which probably neither of us had tried before. It's strange, but had we been put into a full seven-piece band made up of players from seven different countries we would have had a better idea of what to do.

The whole game, in fact, consists of having a reasonable idea in advance of where your particular instrument ought to fit into the general ensemble sound, and then being ready to modify that idea as quickly as possible to match the real sounds you hear around you when the band starts playing. And you do this *while* the band's playing. Rehearsals are very uncommon; partly because rehearsal fees are even more uncommon, but partly because lifelong buskers get to pride themselves on being able to live a bit dangerously and keep a straight face. I remember once waiting to go on as a member of a band which had been cobbled together to accompany the veteran American cornet-player, Wild Bill Davison. The entire preparation for the performance consisted of his turning and saying, semi-seriously, "Now listen, let's get all the hellos over back here. No shaking hands with one another on the bandstand; that kinda thing can make the customers feel uneasy." This brave man had never yet, I think, heard a note from any of us; I have to say that had he done so, *he* might have been feeling uneasy.

Classical musicians used to have a derogatory term: *a telephone orchestra.* Just the same sort of thing, but with a necessary added touch of bitterness. This would be an orchestra consisting of all too many substitutes, assembled by phone and often, in effect, providing the conductor of a concert with a quite different ensemble from the one he'd rehearsed—and whose absent members, incidentally, had been paid for the rehearsals. In the sort of music I'm talking about, though, the title wouldn't be derogatory; all the bands are telephone orchestras.

And that's where the books of phone numbers come in. I said they tended to be eccentric, and so they do. Mostly they're bottom-heavy. It's the bottom of the band, the drummers and bass-players, who rate the most entries. There'll be a fair number of trumpet-players and saxophonists, quite a few pianists, and even the odd trombonist or two; but there'll be page upon page of bassists and drummers. This isn't because there are more of them in existence. It's because you have to ring up more of them before you find one who's free, and willing to turn out. A lot of wheedling has to go on, and there's call for a variety of techniques. Depending on your nerve, you can either play safe, and book your rhythm team months ahead, when a freelance will accept almost any engagement in order to have something, at least, in an empty diary—the risk you take is that something better will turn up in the interim; or you can go for serious brinkmanship, and delay ringing round until teatime on the day of the gig, in the hope of taking one by surprise while feeding or at a moment when he's glad of a reason to be out of the house for the evening. That would happen only very rarely: bass-players work so many nights that their wives tend to be particularly tenacious of the nights they have at home. Or so they say.

If your brinkmanship should fail, you're in trouble, of course. Bands designed to have solid underpinning sound thin and helpless without it, so there's a practical reason for all this tyranny from below. I have to say that it's not as severe as it was a couple of decades ago, when the arrival of rock music and the bass guitar opened things up by increasing the supply of people who could play some sort of bass line. But before that it was a perennial burden, a negative, dissuasive element, like a state censorship or a currency export limit. It was like a left-over wartime shortage.

In those days at least, bass players, and to a slightly lesser extent, drummers, had an image rather like that of the miller in a mediaeval village. They owned expensive, elaborate and essential items of technology; they knew their worth in market terms and drove hard bargains. They could lift you up, and they could let you down. And they never did anything for nothing. If a band was forming, or rehearsing new material, or preparing for a broadcast, the bassist and drummer would always flatly decline to rehearse, on the grounds that *they* didn't need to sweat over the parts like the brass and reed players, thank you very much; so long as the pianist was there to vamp the harmonies, that would do nicely. And they always had another job that night, in some dance band or other. In fact, they often had another job on the nights you thought they were booked with you; it would turn up at short notice, and be better paid. They'd send a dep—no need to rehearse him. No *point* in rehearsing him, either, in some instances.

For there were two types of bassist. There were bass-players, and there were bass-owners. The bass-owners formed a sizable, strange sub-class, which outnumbered the bass-players by about five to one. They were people who had bought a double-bass as an investment, and had learned just enough to make a generalised, fairly rhythmical, low humming or thudding noise on it. Not, you must understand, any actually identifiable notes. They could only get away with it on a low-register instrument. On a trumpet or a clarinet, they would have been rumbled at once, if not actually lynched by audiences; but down among the dead notes, they were on to a good thing. They sounded more or less like those home-made broomstick-and-teachest basses the skiffle groups had in the Fifties, but they looked much more acceptably expensive; in fact some of the basses were really handsome instruments, and their owners often had looks to match. They were what you got on the night your bass-*player* suddenly got a better job. And your gig, in turn, was what they got in return for their investment. They were the millers *par excellence*. They got by without grinding much corn at all. Typical was One-Note-Jack, a tall, doleful man, who hardly moved, once he'd planted his bass and himself at the back of the stand, and was never known to pluck more than the first beat of a four-beat bar.

I talk about these people in the past tense, although there are still quite a few about—even One-Note-Jack, as I was surprised to learn only the other day. I suppose that in the thirty years since I last heard him he's only got through what would be seven-and-a-half-years' notes for a proper bassist, so he may still be feeling quite fresh. But the advent of bass-guitar players did undercut the investment structure somewhat, in that their instruments were rather cheaper to buy and easier to learn to play properly; so they found their way into the dance bands and even into some of the jazz groups, where their comparatively easy-going natures made up in part for the nastiness of the instrument they played. For some reason, too, they were easier to book than either the double-bass players or the double-bass owners. I suspect they're a different breed: failed guitarists, quite a few of them, and of a lighter temperament than men whose first impulse had been to go in low and strong. But they do share one characteristic with their colleagues who use what tends these days to be called the Upright Bass. They all lurk in their dens, waiting to be called on; they're very unlikely to provide work for others, in the way that trumpet players and saxophonists frequently do. And, with the towering and troubled exception of the late Charles Mingus, it's very rare for a good bass player actually to lead a band. Fisher's Fourth Rule of Engagement states that a bassist who offers employment is very unlikely indeed to be proficient, and that the financial incentives must be weighed very carefully against the potential suffering. A splendid example of the sort of man who owns both a bass and a band is the odious Sven Klang, in the film, *Sven Klangs Kvintet*; his way of talking into the microphone while continuing to thud away gives all the warning anyone could need. Mind you, I did have early leanings towards the lower register myself. At my school there was a concept called the School Orchestra, really a random collection of instruments which were periodically issued to keen boys. The idea was that each keen boy should take away his oboe, viola or French horn, somehow learn to play it, and come back ready to be directed into an ensemble by the Music Master. What *he* got out of this annually-repeated pretence I still can't imagine. I know I never heard a sound out of any of the school instruments. Had I been able to get my hands on one, I'd have made a noise on it all right; but I was only a fairly keen—or, more accurately, a fitfully keen—boy, and I was doubly thwarted by the militarism of the place and of the time. The instrument I wanted most of all was the clarinet, but my claim was topped by that of a smart boy who had a louder singing voice, and who was moreover an ornament of the School Air Training Squadron; I believe it was thought that, armed with his clarinet, he could in some way lead a mutation of the Cadets' extremely basic drum-and-bugle band into a full military band, of the sort that has silver saxophones and glockenspiels on sticks.

Plan B was the school double bass. I must have been going through a phase of having a rather mystical attitude to music, and to that instrument in particular; for a start, I couldn't find anybody who had ever seen it. I was an awestruck novice musician, and that meant that I didn't see learning to play as a matter of dexterity, perfectly-absorbed tuition and fidelity to a score; I approached it as a forest of forbidden sounds, never before heard, or even imagined. I thought of the double bass as the deepest repository of the darkest roots of sound. I didn't give a thought to the sheer effort of lugging it about, or building up my wrist muscles on the fingerboard. But where *was* the thing? It was a strongly Christian school, and enough of that had rubbed off to make me understand that you could have faith in the existence of something even if nobody could show it to you. So I believed in the school double bass, lying there among the foundations where it had been stowed at the start of the war four or five years earlier, as a precaution against bombs. Since when the Air Training Corps had built up over its hiding place a stack of their fireproof filing cabinets, secret records and armaments. There existed no protocol by which the stack could be breached. And as an only fitfully-keen boy, I lacked the stamina to lean on the Squadron on my own behalf.

Particularly since I was only a civilian, one of the effete set who elected to spend drill afternoons learning something called Civics from the woolly-mannered, ineffectual-looking Pacifist Master. I now know the Civics to have been a most incisively logical anarchism, and pretty good of its kind; as for the Pacifist Master, he was a Quaker historian, an Oxford don who appeared to have been sentenced to a spell of teaching in our school as a kind of penance, or as war work. If he was a Conscientious Objector, the authorities may well have slyly sent him to our school for the pleasure of seeing him sweating it out in a quasi -military establishment. He certainly did his bit for peace so far as my education went. I could tell he'd made his mark by the way some of the other masters ridiculed him in retrospect as soon as the shooting stopped and he went back to Oxford.

Anyway the school double bass, that musical Moby Dick, was never to surface in my time. Had I managed to get hold of it I might in time have managed to invest in a bass of my own. It could have turned into a nice little earner over the years. But I went home and struggled with our ageing piano. It had playable notes for a couple of octaves above Middle C, but for nearly three octaves going downwards; and I'm left-handed anyway, so I could set myself up for a few years of mysterious growling and banging down there. I was victimised in the end, though: I fell into the clutches of a calculating band-leader who realised I could be tricked into doing the bass-player's job with my left hand as well as my own with my right, all for one man's pay. So he sacked the bass-player. Then I quit. Then he persuaded the guitarist to add the piano chords and the bass line to his own part. He had to contort himself dreadfully in order to do it, of course. I haven't heard of that guitarist for a long time. The band-leader's comfortably off.

§

When I was about eighteen, and something of a veteran in the business of daring to bang out a small repertoire of ill-fingered tunes at jazz sessions around Birmingham, I started to form the idea of early retirement; and before I was twenty, I'd done it. For the first time, anyway. I couldn't imagine that I wasn't soon going to grow out of it. I didn't know I was hooked on this music, and was already part of a network which was spreading quietly and rapidly, particularly at that time, the late Forties: a network made out of something strong, and so extensive that fresh bits of it are still coming into view, even now.

You can see evidences of it in what I think of as a benignly pathological jazz addiction, or provocative, incantatory *naming* of jazz in places where it can't be guaranteed to produce goodwill, though it might. The playwright Alan Plater's a good example of somebody who uses his media-access to wave a jazz flag. The plot of the television series *The Beiderbecke Affair*, which could have started anywhere Plater chose, starts with an order placed by the amiable hero, Trevor Chaplin, for a set of tapes of recordings made by Bix Beiderbecke in the late Twenties. As a character, Trevor Chaplin is a sort of open space—an allotment, perhaps—rather untidily planted with a collection of Alan Plater virtues: innocence; suspicion; feeling; resistance to humbug; general Northerliness; a wary commitment to women; complete commitment to football; complete commitment to jazz. Now the football, for the purposes of run-of-the-mill television drama, would have done on its own; but it's played down in favour of the jazz, which gives the character a touch of irrationality the drama needs. I guess pathological addiction to football on its own wouldn't be thought irrational at all.

But Trevor Chaplin's jazz-addiction isn't the pin-headed, nit-picking specialism which could be offered as the jazz-collector's equivalent of blind loyalty to the home team. For him, the home team is practically the whole of jazz music, from King Oliver to Sonny Rollins, Miles Davis and Toshiko Akiyoshi and Lew Tabackin—all those names he rolls off his tongue as he rummages through the records in Big Al's warehouse. They're all emblazoned on the banner. It's not Swing against Bop, or Blues against Big Bands; it's Jazz in General against Creeping Evil. And it is, as I said, an incantation, a naming of names: not much actual jazz was played in *The Beiderbecke Affair* for all the allusions to jazz in the jolly soundtrack. But the name Beiderbecke is, as anyone familiar with the history and hagiography of jazz knows, no ordinary word. It's a magical one, which works in much the way the name "Gatsby" has come to do, suggesting far more than it denotes.

I picked on The *Beiderbecke Affair* because it's a particularly meritorious example of the injection of a jazz loyalty which is, strictly speaking, somewhat surplus to the requirements of its surroundings. But you can spot others, once you know what you're looking for. There is in Bill Cosby a team loyalty to the work of black jazz musicians which goes a little beyond his general programme of systematically subverting all the old images of black people—whether as devils incarnate or Uncle Tom—by sanitising them into the world of a Middle-American sitcom. He plugs the acknowledged heroes of black achievement, like Count Basie, or Ray Charles, but there's a little extra warmth, a touch of the adolescent with a grown-up cheque book, about the way he makes sure it all gets in the script. And there's the curious matter of Cliff Huxtable's old father. This character is a tame and folksy old fellow, who looks as if he'd be an Uncle Tom if only there were any white folks for him to suck up to; but Cosby makes him a retired jazz trombonist, putting his feet up and dedicating himself to orgies of family piety after what seems to have been a career in a band of really hard men—something like one of the early editions of Art Blakey's Jazz Messengers. I can't imagine Art Blakey himself getting like that; but never mind. The jazz fan in Cosby gets his foot in the door.

They're always doing it. John Wain wrote a jazz novel and some jazz poetry; and although their writings about it occupy separate compartments, away from their poetry and fiction for the most part the way in which jazz fed Philip Larkin and Kingsley Amis from boyhood on is plain to see. The historian Eric Hobsbawm borrowed the name of the black trumpeter Frankie Newton for his critical writings on jazz. And I remember how the novelist Jack Trevor Storey angled to get the American saxophonist and personage Bud Freeman lined up for a part in his fantasy-autobiography on television, only to be foiled by employment regulations.

Then there are the persistent players, the incurable second line; the people whose main career has been in another art, or a profession in which their eminence might not seem consistent with the need to slope off and play in the local jazz club, or drive to distant cities by night, unable to resist a gig. Even without crossing the Atlantic to recruit Woody Allen, you can make the point with better clarinet players. There was the acoustic architect Sandy Brown; there's the cartoonist Wally Fawkes; there's the film critic Ian Christie; there's the artist Alan Cooper. Other names; Alan Davie, painter and avant-garde jazz cellist; Barry Fantoni; Jeff Nuttall; Russell Davies.

Apart from sharing that habit of perpetual truancy into music, I've also gone out of my way to earn a modest place in the complete file of case histories of unwarranted jazz naming. A boyhood hero of mine was the Chicagoan pianist Joe Sullivan. By the mid-Sixties he was an obscure and neglected figure and near the end of his life; his old records weren't getting reissued. While assembling poems for a collection I wrote one—I called it 'The Thing About Joe Sullivan'—which was really my version of what I'd have liked to read as the sleeve note of a new Joe Sullivan album, had there been one. It was about Joe Sullivan, and about my own abiding enthusiasm for his music. And I decided to make it the title poem of the book; not because it typified the whole collection, which it didn't, but because I thought it would be nice for me to see Joe Sullivan's name on the cover of a book. What with the ups and downs and ins and outs of publishing, the book when it finally appeared had a different form and had to have a different title; but I carefully kept that poem back, in case the chance came up again. And some ten years and three books later I remembered it and lifted it out of storage and on to a cover; so that the name of Joe Sullivan forced its way that year into the homes of some hundreds of members of the Poetry Book Society. And on the strength of that I somehow managed to get Granada Television to have the idea of letting me play in a group with Bud Freeman—who actually worked with Joe Sullivan—on a programme where I read my Joe Sullivan poem. So I was one up on Jack Trevor Storey for a few minutes.

All this, though, after retiring at twenty, convinced that a youthful canter was on its last legs. For it had been very much a peer-group activity of a particular late-teenage crowd, born between 1928 and 1930 and young enough to miss being called up while the war was still on. Almost without exception we were at, or just leaving, one of about five of the city's Grammar Schools; one or two went into National Service at eighteen, but most seemed to hang around for years on student deferments or with medical disabilities which didn't show themselves in civilian life.

We could tell we were a generation on our own just by the feel of things. It may have been different in all those other towns where, unknown to us at first, something of the kind was simultaneously going on; but the Birmingham crowd developed with a clear feeling of having no predecessors. We knew nobody at all older than ourselves who had ever tried to do what we were trying to do to rescue what was in fact a brief quarter-century of jazz history, not just by collecting records but by actually playing the stuff. In fact, most of us didn't know any older musicians at all. We behaved as if playing music had just been invented. We did know some older record collectors, just back from the war, and they were our first real audiences and our first promoters; but the actual musicians of that generation, who had spent the late Thirties and early Forties keeping up with the latest styles, were back in town making good money in dance bands, and, so far as the music went, disappearing fast into Bebop, where we couldn't have followed them even if we'd wanted to. We didn't even want to try Swing, let alone Bebop. In our crowd of young antiquarians I was regarded as quaintly modernistic, in that I was trying to copy styles popular from the late Twenties to the mid-Thirties, and was worrying my way dangerously towards the edge of the abyss, which was supposed to have opened up some time in 1936, after which everything was plunged into corruption: my purist friends planted their allegiances safely at the beginning of recorded time—acoustically recorded, that is, through enormous megaphone-like horns. But then, they weren't going in for half measures; and I was, strenuously. It's something to do with my character. I figured we had a good deal in common with the nicely brought-up young white boys from Chicago who had been bowled over in the Twenties by the black music from New Orleans, and I thought they should be our models; with more rigorous logic, my friends marched straight to the much more common conclusion, and tried very hard to believe they *were* black men from New Orleans.

Not that those older local musicians—they were mostly about twenty-five—were on speaking terms with any of us at that time. Later on, some of us learned to play just about well enough to keep up with them, as well as moderating our own archaic tastes; and a few of them gave way with advancing years to a little nostalgia for the records and the tunes of their youth, so we met halfway. But mostly they must, on the odd occasions when they heard us filling in as intermission bands, or on carnival floats, have been appalled and disgusted by our impassioned primitivism. By our turnout, too. With demob suits, know-how and a few fiddled clothing coupons, they could manage to look quite smart: loud check jackets with padded shoulders, dark trousers, light tan shoes, wide ties, shirts in interesting colours. Whereas we were reduced by need to what our ideology led us towards anyway, the dress of poor, off-duty cotton-pickers: open-necked white shirt, grey flannels, battered black shoes. The only leeway for personal style was in the size of your wristwatch, and whether you wore it facing outward or round on the inside of your wrist.

Really farouche was the brief vogue for wearing a straight-necked jersey *inside* the shirt, so that a triangle of it showed at the V, T-shirt fashion. Two snags to that. One was that wool was so hard to come by—a typical source was unpicking and dyeing wartime Balaclava helmets—that nobody's mother was ever going to knit a jersey other than the standard sleeveless V-neck, suitable for wearing with a collar and tie; the second was that wearing a jersey under your shirt tickles terribly. The first snag could be partially overcome: you wore your V-neck jersey back-to-front under your shirt. There was a snag to that of course: if you took off your Utility, non-fitted Harris-tweed-type jacket, the V of your jumper, plunging suggestively between your shoulder-blades, showed through your shirt. About the other snag, the tickling, there was nothing at all to be done. I suffered so much that I soon gave up the fancy. But my fellow-pianist Ray Foxley, who, if I remember rightly, introduced it, never seemed troubled—having in any case an eloquent Adam's apple, an expressively-raised chin and an unruffled faraway look. Besides, he was actually being the late Jelly-Roll Morton at the time. The piano-playing was already very like Morton's, and we were on the lookout for the arrival of the personal trademarks—the astrakhan-collared overcoat, the diamond rings, the diamond in the front tooth—even if they would have looked odd on the bus from Bromsgrove. I don't think Jelly-Roll Morton, even in his years of neglect, ever wore his jumper inside his shirt.

All in all, then, it seemed to be a matter of temporary lifestyle rather than the first stage of a career in music, professional or semi-professional, for any of us. We didn't fit either of those categories: we were amateurs, and no doubt about it. We played to try to match the noises in our heads, or our gramophones, and what anybody else made of it was *their* lookout. At first, they told us to stop; later, they'd tolerate us; much later, some of them would pay some of us—and that would take us over the line into the strange world of semi-professionalism, which simply means that you get paid for playing, but not often enough to make a living at it.

But around 1950, the original amateur gang was scattering and nothing seemed to be moving forward. Retirement seemed attractive. The young lady I was walking out with at the time—she played the viola—caught me listening to a Sidney Bechet record and said it was animal, the voice of depravity. Impressed, I retired there and then, and took up poetry which at least *looked* clean. Then she dropped out of my life—actually got a doctor's note; that was enterprising. But I stayed in retirement for a year or two. Then *I* started playing again, whenever I couldn't help it; and I've carried on ever since. And still, whenever I get access to one of the media, I slip in a plug for Joe Sullivan.

§

My very first public performance as a pianist was also one of the rare occasions when I've been billed as a band-leader; I've quite often had my name attached to a trio, but that's just a result of the quaint convention by which pianists are supposed to be the leaders of rhythm sections. Anybody who thinks that should try it sometime. It's a misconception similar to the one which leads people—promoters and club managers more often than not—to come up and engage a band's pianist in conversation, on the grounds that, unlike the players with their eyes shut and things stuck in their mouths, he's not doing anything with his head. As the song doesn't have it, I'd rather *not* lead a band.

But here's how I came to be the leader of Roy Fisher and his Students of Jazz. The school I went to wasn't one of those with a strong jazz cell, enough people to form a six-piece band; my year had a trombonist and a banjo-player; there was a pianist a couple of years ahead of me, who gave it up to become a high-powered scientist; there was another pianist a couple of years behind me, and a drummer as well. Both became professors, but didn't give it up. In fact, they're still at it.

So: we were thin on the ground, and too many of us were pianists. But there was also Horseface. Nobody called him that, and it didn't have much relation to what he looked like; it was just a name he'd have liked to be called, instead of Leslie. This whim was the only illogicality about him, for Horseface was an extremely sensible boy; he got more done than most of us but strode through his adolescence with an awesome sense of his own limitations. He was a good artist, and trained as a painter, but wouldn't paint, for some sound reason or other; he was an excellent mechanic and knew all about cars, but certainly wouldn't be such a madman as to drive one; he was—how can I put it?—formidably celibate, in all directions, under the stern law of his sense of self-preservation. He also knew a great deal about jazz, and was a very enthusiastic and perceptive hand with a gramophone; and somewhere along the line he'd managed to become a very tidy trumpet-player. What he did with this accomplishment was odd, though; he spent his Saturday evenings, crammed into an ancient-looking dress suit, playing third trumpet in Jack Bradney's Dance Orchestra in some Black Country Baths Ballroom or other. But he wouldn't venture on jazz—not on the instrument anyway; if you could have taken down his excitable conversation about Louis Armstrong or Roy Eldridge, and processed it through a trumpet, you'd have had jazz all right. It was as if he knew too much about it to want to do it for himself; the exact opposite of the standpoint of our amateur mob. The less we knew, the keener we were. And Horseface really belonged with us, and not with the Saturday-night semi-pros he earned his pocket-money with.

For a time, I thought his resistance was going to crack. In addition to working in the big band, he had also come by a regular engagement with a strange four-piece dance band. As well as himself, it consisted of a pale young commercial artist on clarinet and saxophone, who wanted to play jazz; a nice lady called Auntie Ivy Tonks, who was in fact the clarinet-player's aunt, on piano; and on drums, a breezy, rather old young man who was like something out of Surtees by way of the wartime RAF—as an update, you could add Basil Brush. He was quite well-to-do, but seemed to have a heavy hormone build-up, and liked to lay about himself and kick up a bit of a racket on his drum-kit; so *he* might be ready to fall into jazz, too. I rather think Auntie Ivy was out of all this, and probably kept getting better offers besides; at any rate, Horseface persuaded himself that I'd taught myself enough piano to help out with the band in her absence. This wasn't true. I was fifteen, and my total experience consisted of about a year of messing about with three chords in the keys of C and F. And I could think of no way in which I could explain to my parents that I was going to go out into the adult world after dark, dressed in a borrowed waiter's outfit; indeed, there was no way of raising the subject of my going out into that world at all. But one summer evening I did manage to slip away to join a practice with the three others.

It was the first time I'd ever heard a dance band, live, and the surroundings were extraordinary. The drummer was heir to a medium-sized factory, in a back street near the city centre, and the band rehearsed in the works canteen. I've forgotten what the factory produced, but the sensations of trailing through the deserted works, up and down rickety wooden stairs in the warm evening sunlight are still with me; and the thought of the particular degree of tunelessness of the canteen piano brings back the agreeably overpowering scent of sawdust and oil which filled the entire place. The other overpowering thing was the colossal din the drummer produced the moment he started to play. I could see his enormously cheery, handlebar-moustachioed face above the flailing cymbals, floating above this agony of noise, which was magnified and mangled by the bare walls of the canteen.

It didn't take me long to prove to the others that I wasn't yet ready to be exposed to people who knew a Veleta from a St. Bernard's Waltz, and that I probably never would be. But they wanted to make use of me for something. The first thing they did was to let me take part in a private recording session, at the drummer's expense. To record, even if you had to pay for it, was still a most romantic thing to do. The domestic tape recorder was still nearly ten years in the future, and there was nothing casual about it. You were recorded direct on to a single-sided soft acetate disc. Each tune cost a pound; each copy cost a pound. This was at a time when the 78s we collected cost five-and fourpence-halfpenny; so your own vanity, if you bought a copy of what you'd recorded, was pushing you into rating yourself at seven or eight times what you'd layout on Duke Ellington or Art Tatum. Moreover, the records were so delicate that if you played them with an ordinary needle it would instantly plough the music off the disc in thin coils of black swarf, so you had to get expensive trailer needles; even so, the things wore out pretty quickly.

Our session was in what turned out to be a converted front bedroom over Mr. Jackman's radio shop in Birchfield Road, Lozells. I finished my homework early, and cycled down there, prepared to record six tunes. This was at least two more tunes than I knew; but I was willing to stretch a point. It was something of a relief for me to find a second pianist there—or, rather, to find that *I* was the second pianist. George, a very snazzy young player who did in fact go on to distinguish himself in the profession, but hadn't at that time got further than being one of Auntie Ivy's occasional deps, had just had his call-up papers, and the session had been hastily rededicated as a wake to George's youth. He knew all the tunes. But I was to be allowed to do two.

Mr Jackman's bedroom had a shiny black baby grand, and that fascinated me more than the recording equipment; I'd never been allowed to get my hands on anything like that before. George, with sleek American hair—no parting, no short back and sides, and rimless Glenn Miller glasses, sat before it as if he'd just taken it out of his monogrammed music-case and fitted it together. A pleasant young lady sitting in the corner, whom I'd taken to be George's girl-friend, was introduced as his sister, and a trained soprano into the bargain. With George accompanying, she recorded a couple of light operatic items, and did them very nicely. Obviously it was for this sort of thing that Mr Jackman had set up his studio. He made a good job of it. When the band struck up, though, he was out of his depth at once; he clearly could see no reason why anybody should want to preserve this kind of noise. Moreover there was the problem of balancing the sound so that the drums might at least seem not to be drowning all the other instruments. In that small room, their volume was even more terrifying.

Apart from that, the music went on to its discs quite tidily. After listening to the playbacks, George and his sister left. Had he stayed, George might have been able to put me right on a couple of things I didn't know I didn't know. The first number we did was an impromptu slow blues. I could handle that: the three chords I was getting by with were the chords of the twelve-bar blues anyway, and I think we did quite well. It was a thrill. The other tune was 'Honeysuckle Rose', which was one of the tunes I believed I knew. My job was to accompany a trumpet and a clarinet playing the tune in near unison in the key of F. My ear had told me the first chord I needed to play wasn't F major; it must be one of the other two chords I believed existed. It isn't. But I chose one of my Flat-Earth Society chords, and banged it out for four solid bars every time it came round. It was B Flat Seventh. I also played it for the whole of the middle eight. Those who are not musicians need to be told only that these actions were very misguided indeed, and are still on my conscience, even though erased from the record, literally, by the scratching of needles, forty years since. It wasn't even an innocent ignorance: I'd got hold of the music, but had refused to believe it. G Minor Eleventh? C Thirteenth? Whose leg were they trying to pull?

My harmonies weren't the only blemish. After the opening ensemble, with its hints of Charles Ives, I had a solo piano chorus. Although continuing to use my wrong chords, I couldn't clash with anybody else, being on my own; I just seemed to be playing a different tune altogether. I also got excited, and speeded up dangerously. Then came a drum solo by the founder of the feast. It was loud, naturally. And it started at the speed I'd reached, and quickly accelerated even further. I forgot to mention that the drummer had a little red MG. The solo bore no relation to the shape of the tune; there was no way of knowing where to come in again. The closing ensemble was nasty, brutish and short. Another pound gone. And a very long three minutes.

We acknowledged the playback as pretty lifelike. It didn't occur to anybody to have a whip-round to raise a pound for another attempt. That was how we sounded, and we didn't know how to do anything about it. I couldn't afford a copy of the record; and besides, the pickup on my 1920s acoustic gramophone was so heavy that it shredded even ordinary records. I heard it only once more, about a year later. In the interim, I'd accepted conversion to the correct changes to 'Honeysuckle Rose', and was glad the record was already wearing out. The copy was the drummer's own, and he'd been listening to his solo a good deal. The blues side wasn't much worn. I wish I still had that.

I'd also, in that intervening year, tasted blood as a band-leader. I didn't taste much, and it didn't taste good. The band had decided to release me to the public as the leader of a band-within-a-band. The concept followed that of Bob Crosby's Bobcats, Woody Herman's Woodchoppers, Tommy Dorsey's Clambake Seven and the Benny Goodman Sextet: all the big bands had one. But not many four-piece bands did. The Harmonaires, or whatever the quartet called itself, was possibly unique in the audacity by which it transformed itself before the audience's very eyes, into Roy Fisher and his Students of Jazz. This was done simply by removing Auntie Ivy from the piano stool and substituting me, looking suitably studious behind my glasses, and with a black bow in place of my school tie. It all happened as part of the works dance and beano of the drummer's family factory; and I was released from the protection of my family for the evening in the care of Horseface, whose craggy manner and frequent loud protestations made it clear, even to my mother, that he did not Go With Girls. So off we went from the factory gates one Autumn evening in a string of coaches to a strange pub in a spot about thirty miles away which I didn't know at all. The Nautical William was one of those

Thirties Art-Deco buildings, white, with bevelled corners; it just seemed to have materialised out of the dark for one night, and, not knowing where it was, I never expected to see it again. But driving down the road from Bridgnorth to Kidderminster not long ago, I spotted it: aged a bit, but still having its own strange name, and not, so far at least, retitled 'Naughtys'—or maybe 'Willies'. Or both.

It was quite a heady evening out. My mother didn't go to works beanos, or she would have known that the scenes among which Horseface habitually passed unscathed were even more appalling than Going With Girls; amounting at times even to what would have to be called Going With Grown Women. I'd lived with unblinking eyes through the VE Night party in our street, and I knew I could take it. There was a cabaret, with heavily painted ladies, and a blue comedian in a cream tuxedo; there was dancing, and there was drinking. Our bit, when it came, was quite painless. The Students of Jazz played their unimaginable version of 'Honeysuckle Rose' as heard on record; I played a solo version of Meade Lux Lewis's 'Bear Cat Crawl', but cut it short because I couldn't hear myself for the din of people chattering. Then the Students of Jazz reassembled for their last number ever: 'Big Noise from Winnetka', a piece popular at the time, and consisting only of a simple workout for bass, drums and whistling through the teeth. We had no bass; trumpet, clarinet and piano played the whistling bit; and the drummer went on and on, and up and up. *Kazam. Pow. Splat.* The End. He was Head of the Drawing Office as well as the boss's son; it went down very well. Somebody gave me a pound note, and I gave up band-leading.

It was the end for the Harmonaires, as well. A short while later I called on Horseface to see how things were going. He indicated, by a short expressive mime, that the drummer had found a new outlet for his hormone build-up in female form, and would never need to drum again. I don't know what form his turn at the annual works beanos took after that.

§

The deepest dive I ever played in was the Crevasse Club in Birmingham. It had a few other names in its short life, all of them to do with plumbing depths of one sort or another; but that one catches its character well enough. I didn't even know of its existence before one Monday evening in the spring of 1964, when the tenor sax player on a one-nighter in a perfectly healthy-looking, almost deserted upstairs room went broody inside his neat Italian-style dark blue suit. "Um. Ah," he said. "We're starting off down the Dreaded Crevasse on Saturday. Would you care to do it?" He was a very good tenor player, decidedly ahead of my league, and the bass-player and drummer he said he'd invited were as good as anybody in town, so I was interested. "What's it about?" I said; "And where is it, and what time?" "Well, it's a sort of downstairs drinking club down the back of the Fruit Market. They want us every Saturday from two till about five." "Two till five a.m.? What are they paying?" "No, no, it's afternoon. I dunno about the money; but he says we can have whatever food and drink we want."

All of that was unusual enough to get me out and into my mini-van without any lunch, the following Saturday. The instructions for finding the club had been complex, and didn't seem to help much. At that time on a Saturday the markets in the area down by Jamaica Row were winding down, and the district was a wilderness of broken cartons, dropped cauliflowers, trodden tomatoes and paper blowing about everywhere in a keen spring breeze. It was a district of big halls and warehouses, and nothing in the way of shops or restaurants; and although it was a place I knew quite well, it was almost devoid of names and signs. It didn't look promising. And it also looked deeply wrong as a place and a time for playing subterranean music.

I parked the van between heaps of vegetable refuse, and set off exploring, after locking it with particular care. Not that there was much point in locking those early minis at all. People used to lean on the door handles and pop the locks, sometimes slipping a pocket-sized length of pipe over the handles so as to increase the leverage. I comforted myself with the thought that it was broad daylight, and Digbeth Police Station was only just round the corner.

When I found the Crevasse Club, which I did a few minutes later by chasing after a double-bass which I saw disappearing up an alleyway, the thought of the police station became less reassuring. It all looked very illegal—and in a stagy sort of way, too. The alleyway, running behind a row of derelict houses, was impressively foul, with all the customary props strewn about: dustbins, chip-papers, cans, the odd car-tyre; a slow trickle of some fluid or other underfoot. The scruffy brickwork seemed to have no mortar left, but a single door in it had been painted fairly recently. It was heliotrope, but had no identifying marks. And there was no sound.

The bass-player and I stood there, looking for a knocker or a bell. There wasn't even a handle. "Any special knock? No. Here goes." We hammered. And again. The door swung open, and we were in, with the door shut behind us. It was a very small dark bar, completely jammed with people; underfoot there was a brick floor. "That way down gentlemen," said whoever had let us in. "Your friends are waiting for you."

With a bit of persuasion the crowd parted to let us through to the top of a flight of steps, blocked with some more crowd. Down that; and immediately down another flight, and so into a strange chamber at the bottom of it all, where the real crowd was. Not that it was waiting for us. It seemed to have plenty of amusements of its own to be getting along with. There was a piano, and a corner for us to play in, so we got ourselves together, and played a set. Everybody seemed to be happy.

Before, behind, between, above and below the customers, it was possible to work out what sort of place we were in, and what had been happening to it. We were in a small suite of dank cellars and sub-cellars and cubby-holes, the storage spaces underneath some old shop; and it had all been subjected to a right going-over. Nothing cosy or tasteful; not a whiff of flock wallpaper or Dralon. A kind of geological mutation was in progress; not finished, because in odd corners you could still see the raw edges of its creation. It was obviously done by hand. Somebody had lined the whole place with rough swags of wire-netting: pinned it to the walls, rounded out the corners, made mummy-wrappings round the brick pillars that held up the low ceilings. And a laborious crinkly coating of stiff white mush—Plaster of Paris, Polyfilla, something of that kind—had been added to the wire-netting, layer on layer, with miniature stalactites of the stuff hanging in petrified festoons overhead. Wherever you tried to move, the structure itself was crouching over you, lunging out at you, snapping off, coming off and whitening your clothes. There were a few little spotlights fixed in deep tunnels in the icing, just enough to show up the ghostly, shapeless whiteness, among which, oddly, were traces of bamboo. There was an uneven cellar floor, mostly concrete and fairly dry; and the furniture was a job lot of barrel-tables and padded casks to sit on.

As a place to play it had its points. There was no need for microphones, for the environment was of itself an amplifier; indeed, I suppose it looked rather like an enlarged version of one of those polystyrene medical models of the inside of the human ear, with curving passages and strange chambers. And surprisingly, the piano wasn't bad. But then, it hadn't been there long. Its position wasn't calculated to be good for its health; and in the three or four months of our Saturday-afternoon residency it was to age rapidly. It sat on a damp concrete floor, and in the wall just behind it was the extractor fan, which sucked down to the lowest level of the establishment all the fumes of alcohol and tobacco and vented them somewhere into those streets behind the market. Before hitting the fan, those fumes were vigorously drawn, as through a filter, through the body of the piano—and of the pianist. There was a good deal of cider-drinking among the young and arty in those days, and with a sizable West Indian presence, an awful lot of "Rumanblack"—rum, with blackcurrant cordial—went down. Even worse than all the smoke and booze vapours was the heavy, descending breath of whatever was being cooked two floors up, in what had been the old shop and was now a blacked-out coffee-bar-cum-beefburger-and-chips-dispenser. There were also various hashes, and sundry chutneys and pickles; and there was a great deal of blue smoke. I can't remember which of the club's personnel was to blame for all this. I think they took it in turns; there was certainly no chef. Whatever the source of the odours, a fair proportion of them always ended up as the same indistinguishable cocktail clogging my clothing, most of which had to go straight into the washer when I got home. And it was only on the first Saturday that I took advantage of the free food. After that I used to spend the intermissions going up for air.

In spite of the smack of illegality the club had, the police didn't raid it. I suppose they were there anyway, among the rather bohemian clientele. It was obvious that our Saturday sessions were designed to run from the time the pubs had to shut to the time they could open again at five-thirty, at which point the customers would move on to somewhere where the drinks were cheaper. While it lasted, it was a scene; it was where it was at. Most of the denizens of the city centre would turn up there sooner or later, and jabber away at one another over our noise, or that of the sitters-in, who came in increasing numbers and took over our jobs in the intervals, which got longer and longer as the weeks went by. Sometimes I'd be relieved at the keyboard by Little Stevie, who was about fourteen and shouldn't have been let in. He grew up very quickly to be Steve Winwood; he said little, and certainly didn't sing at all; but he had great stamina and many, many well-directed fingers. If he came to sit in, I'd stay and listen; otherwise it was out into the air, or up to the coffee bar where, if nobody was cooking up a whole mess of trouble on the stove, you could watch the only Scopitone in the Midlands—it was a French video jukebox, and very catchy. Pop videos still had a fresh, under-produced charm, like pre-war American soundies; and there are quite hard middle-aged men in Birmingham who can still hallucinate the Françoise Hardy item from that Scopitone.

One thing you didn't get in the Crevasse was anxious philosophising from the proprietor, a serious occupational hazard with clubs— particularly clubs which are obviously going to be short-lived. The Crevasse was owned by a pair of affable and slightly bemused brothers whose real livelihood was in some other line, like fruit machines. In the movie, the senior brother might have been played by Laird Cregar, the younger by Robert Mitchum—but that's only to say that the elder needed to wear very large spreads of dark suiting and had teeth that showed quite pearly under his little moustache, while the younger tended towards crumpled grey suits and had eyes that didn't open all the way; at least, not both at the same time. Why they owned it, I don't know. They owned it in the spirit in which people own ramshackle allotment huts or used-furniture repositories piled to the leaky ceilings with broken gas cookers and hospital bedside cabinets. Maybe they'd won it, or had it in payment for a debt. It was a club in a perpetual state of Becoming.

Indeed I once witnessed the actual process of Becoming. This was about the time I had the club positively vetted. One day in the Kardomah, my friendly Building Society Manager and Marxist Justice of the Peace laid down his *Daily Telegraph* and gave me a fatherly look. "I have information," he said, "that you are becoming involved with the activities of the Crevasse Club. The Brothers." "What's the warning?" I asked. "I don't know," he said. "I don't know. But, for the present—watch it. I will check it out." The checking took a week or two. Then "You'll be relieved to learn," he told me, "that according to my informants, the Crevasse Club and the Brothers are blameless. There is nothing on them." I was surprised, rather than relieved: I should have thought the Brothers would be down for wasting police time by consistently acting in a suspicious manner, and running a deceptively disorderly house. I called in one weekday afternoon to collect some records which had been left there for me. The club was shut, but not inactive, as it turned out. I was let in by the Robert Mitchum brother, who was holding a little jam-jar of something white. He led me down the stairs to where he was happily creating decor, poking wet plaster on to a new stretch of chicken wire. In the room was a young local band-leader who had just struck lucky, gone professional, and was starting to do his bit of social drinking out of hours as if his very lifestyle depended on it; and there was a table of quiet businessmen.

As I chatted to the band-leader, and the brother plastered, two young women with big shopping bags came down the stairs, in outdoor clothes. They looked like new barmaids, and we forgot they were there. A minute later there came a couple of short, disjointed blasts of Easy-Listening music; and there they were, bent over a little portable tape recorder. "OK," said the brother, and went on plastering his chicken-wire. The young women started the tape again, looked at each other, looked away, and took their coats off. Then, taking care not to catch anybody's eye, they took their dresses off, pretty briskly, and laid them on their shopping bags. The businessmen looked up in dismay, and pretended not to notice. "It's just an audition," said the brother, carefully shaping a drip into a stalactite. The girls were each already out of a layer of fancy underwear, but appeared to have several more layers to go. It was starkly embarrassing; even more so when the tape ran out before the first tune was through, and one of them tripped across, head well down, to turn it over. The band-leader and I made no excuses but left, with the businessmen not far behind. Cabaret Time at the Crevasse never really came to anything.

And the Saturday afternoon crushes came to a sudden stop quite soon. One Saturday in August I turned up to find the tenor player standing in the alley in front of the shut door. "It's all off," he said. "There's been a flood. The cellar's full up. We'd be... potholing." There was no knowing what the flood was of; I thought of the piano under a dark swirl of cider, rum-and-blackcurrant, seepage from the precarious toilets on the stairs, with sodden white plaster crumbling off to cloud the waters, and the odd swimming rat taking refuge on its lid. "Anyway," said the tenor player, "they'll give me a ring when it's dried out again."

Not unexpectedly, there was no such call. But about a year later a nice young man who owned a double-bass and was new in town rang me and asked me to do an evening session there. All was quiet; all was dry. The piano had a few stains, and it sounded a little throaty, a little distant and reproachful. Very few people in; which was as well, for the band was ragged. As for the club, it was in a kind of posthumous trance. And a few weeks later the Brothers moved to an existing but languishing club on the top floor of an office-block a couple of miles out of town. It was well above flood level, and they didn't redecorate it. Indeed, they never even opened the curtains.

II

ROY FISHER
ON ROY FISHER

POET ON WRITING

I'm either writing—physically making a creature of blackish marks on whitish paper—or I'm not. At such times I'm willing to admit that I'm a poet, but at others the persona doesn't exist. It's almost unthinkable for me to experience the arrival of what I recognise as the movement or form of a poem simply as a mental or a vocal thing. I have first to be setting words down and shifting them about in my inhibited, brain-wrenching, left-handed script. It may well be that when I write I use, as a formal constraint, the residue of the early difficulty I had over learning to hold a pen and move it across the paper in an unnatural direction. I'm a glib and garrulous talker, given to branching sentences that forget their own beginnings; but in order to get me to write them down, word-patterns have to have at least a claim on permanency. And it's in the time of their being turned into marks that they make themselves audible to me: then I hear the chime of a phrase back and forth along its length. The muttering voice—which isn't quite mine—in my head speaks them, and sometimes I'll sound them aloud. Always, before passing a version as final.

Exceptions to all this are burlesque or sarcastic pieces like 'Paraphrases', 'The Neglect of Figure Composition' or 'A Modern Story', which are elaborations of jokes which turned up unbidden in everyday life, as reactions to or summations of something that was going on. They tend to be composed, polished and performed in the head, then just written down, rather than written.

The comic pieces mostly have characters, situations, mimetic voices, whereas the poems are very short on anecdote, drama, moralised incidents; often lacking, so I'm told, any presence of myself as a character, or recognisable manikin. This has to be true. I don't see a poem of mine as a setting for myself as a character, a composition which can in some sense contain me; instead it's something found and formed within my boundaries and then, maybe, projected out into the language-exchange to try its luck. This view drastically affects the way I compose. For while my relations with other people are—or so they seem to me—extremely simple for the most part, and certainly not likely to generate much in the way of paperwork, my relations with my own inner life are complex, shifting and bulky, and over several decades they've produced a great heap of notebooks and journals. Although this mass of observations, sensations and introspections is inchoate, and undeveloped except by the movements of its own tides, I've come to think of it, rather than the poems, as my work, my central occupation. It's supremely useless to anyone but me. It doesn't progress towards becoming a system. It gives an air of fitful authority, as if somebody had dropped the contents of the *I Ching* and then stuffed them back together haphazardly. Indeed, I use it as a disorderly private oracle. I can move about in it, guided by its skeins of metaphors, elliptical jargon and obsessively-acquired images, and most of the recurrent tones and images of my finished poems have first identified themselves to me by the way they feature insistently in the notebooks.

Sometimes I've lifted material out quite soon after its collection and used it with little modification. The prose sections of 'City' were taken from entries only briefly stored, used in an abortive work, then reused at once in the published one. 'A Furnace', another assembled work, is made out of the interactions of ideas and images which had been waiting for periods ranging from a few months to nearly twenty-five years. Whatever poetic that piece has derives from the conviction that those heterodox materials belonged together and needed an idiom that would allow that to come about.

It's rare for the notebooks to offer any ready-worded passages. I keep the writing there fairly loose and allusive, probably so that I'll not be tempted for sociable reasons to publish it as finished work when I'm short of things to send to editors. I'm not the kind of writer who has a compulsion to compose and publish continually, so as to bear witness to the fact that the sensibility's alive and well. (I think my work as a jazz piano-player takes care of that: an extra ten choruses of *Stella by Starlight* can dispose of any pressure of that sort that may be building up.) Another reason for the less-than-written style of the notebooks is my intention that they should share properties of mutability with memory, imagination, dreams and involuntary insights, and so remain part of the fluid medium of my inner life.

I work on the assumption that life has what I called earlier its own tides: tendencies to movement which are, or resemble, observable natural laws. To make poems I trail static things into the current to see what shapes they set up. Chance stimuli have always worked better for me than deliberate ones, and I've used many kinds as foci for concentration. Phrases picked at random, not necessarily by me, from newspapers, or thrown up by someone else's automatic writing (almost all the poems in 'City'—even the wholly anecdotal 'The Entertainment of War'—and many others from that period); paintings, news photographs, movie stills ('Five Morning Poems', 'Interiors'). There was a period when I found action-photographs, with their exaggerated fixity of frozen motion, particularly productive in creating reactive imaginative movements which I hadn't foreseen. *The Ship's Orchestra* came as an oblique and distant response to a print of Picasso's *Three Musicians* which I had in my room. It was also, as a manuscript object, a sensuous response to a certain wad of blank quarto paper, grey-lined and with red margins, which I'd had charge of while invigilating an exam and which I took home afterwards. 'The Cut Pages' was likewise set going by the paper it was to be written on, paper which was asking to be saved from a curse it had fallen under; 'Wonders of Obligation' came into being to inhabit its destined, pre-described home, a given number of pages of a given size and a particular paper.

The way *The Ship's Orchestra* text was written illustrates a characteristic method of mine. I hardly ever, even in long works, block ideas in advance, or plant phrases up ahead to work my way towards. As a general rule, when I know, from a sense of imaginative freedom, the feeling of ideas coming easily to hand, that I'm going to be able to compose, I quieten language down to zero: a blank page and a silence in the head. Then when the words start to come I make the text with a very simple forward progression, aiming to bring each section to a finished state as I go. Not a lapidary technique, allowing for later substitutions; more like fresco painting, where images quickly become fixed and unalterable. As the work proceeds, every new line or patch has its nature guided by the whole of what's gone before, and, preferably by no other factors.

When I started out, the conceiving and making of verses seemed to me a matter of the utmost difficulty, and ever since, except when teaching rudiments to others, I've managed to plot myself a path which has borne this impression out. Consequently, since my poems are hard for me to find, or come to me only by devious ways, I like to use only the simplest verbal techniques in their making. I absorbed the stern instructions of Pound, Zukofsky and Bunting quite early on, and they're still there. Unless I particularly want to produce density I go for an open texture, feeling for a sense of conceptual space in which a reader might possibly perceive the elements of the poem hanging or floating, ready to be related one to another. (This basic piece of consideration, combined with an ear for how the poem should be paced when read aloud, constitutes the whole of my awareness of an audience, or readership.) When I judge there's enough heterogeneity, so that more material would cause the work to fissure or buckle in on itself, then I stop. If it's a sectional work I stop the section; if it's a single poem I end the poem. And then, apart from worrying at the odd phrase which I haven't managed to tune to my satisfaction as I've gone along, it's all done. My redrafts aren't undertaken for comparison or study. They're simply manuscript copyings, done in order to get an intimate knowledge of what I've done, so that the need for a minor alteration will show up as a discomfort in the copying. From my mid-twenties nearly all this work has been done in hard-covered exercise-books, partly because I like the feel of them, partly as a precaution against the loss of loose sheets. I don't take a text to the word-processor until I need copies of it. By that stage it will have nothing more to tell me, and I'm unlikely to look at it again till I meet it at a reading.

NOTE ON *THE CUT PAGES*

Some of these pieces supplement the other prose I have published: *The Ship's Orchestra,* and parts of *City.*

The earliest are the two 'Hallucinations', which date from 1959. As printed here they are taken from rather longer versions which appeared in 1962 in the Migrant Press tailpiece to *City,* called 'Then Hallucinations': this pamphlet was reprinted in the magazine *Kulchur* in the same year.

The 'Stopped Frames and Set Pieces' were written in 1964, after *The Ship's Orchestra.* They are renderings of some items from a large collection of old newspaper and magazine photographs and bits of film which I had a few years earlier made into a narrative collage like a movie. Many of the pictures I had were obvious descendants of Muybridge's sequences— or rather of single items from them: the movement-sequences broken into separate fragments the eye cannot record, while the machine can; unknown forms and dispositions which, when caught and printed, ask to be read like any other form. The work I did with them has some relation to Robbe-Grillet's *Instantanés,* which I had not then seen; but I think I was after something different. 'The Flight Orator' comes from the same period, and is a sort of aria which arose from, and then immediately swamped, a short story in the realistic mode I was trying to write.

The other two sections of the book are improvisations done this year. *The Cut Pages* was written on sheets taken out of a notebook between whose covers I no longer wanted to work. The aim in the improvisation was to give the words as much relief as possible from serving in planned situations; so the work was taken forward with no programme beyond the principle that it should not know where its next meal was coming from.

It was unable to anticipate, but it could have on the spot whatever it could manage to ask for. This method produced very rapid changes of direction. The process in the 'Metamorphoses' *is* a much slower one. They are exercises in changing, in full view, one thing into another whose nature was quite unforeseen at the outset, the change to be worked by playing over the starting idea until it began to loosen and dissolve, and yield place to another which looked as if it had a right to be there. The point of interest for me here was not so much the ideas as the sloweddown exploration of the kind of field in which ideas exist, and the ways they have of succeeding one another.

Roy Fisher writes...

The Thing About Joe Sullivan is a collection of poems written since the appearance of *Matrix* in 1971. The only earlier piece is the title poem, which I wrote in 1965 but left unpublished for a long while because it was something of an oddity among the rest of my work: although I was playing jazz for five or six years before I started writing poetry I have never been interested in works made of jazz combined with poetry and I have written about the music only very rarely. This particular piece is a fan's poem. Joe Sullivan was a Chicagoan pianist of prodigious energy and great, if erratic, expressive power. He was not one of the great innovators and is now too little remembered; but it was from listening to his recordings that I took some early lessons in imaginative opportunism and I have had no difficulty in staying loyal to what I learned. Sullivan died seven years ago and the book is dedicated to his memory.

There's a musical element, albeit a suppressed one, in the sequence 'Handsworth Liberties'. I hope the poems have a presence of their own, but readers might be interested to learn how they came to be composed. I have elsewhere told how, for one reason and another, almost the whole of my childhood and youth passed in the suburb where I was born, with only a couple of brief holidays and no extended journeys; consequently I came to know the place with an almost oppressive intimacy, and anything which I read or heard and which made a strong impression on me was liable to be translated into local images. I saw nothing strange in the fact that many pieces of music which I had first listened to in adolescence were always accompanied on subsequent hearings by the visual images of particular suburban spots and vistas, each apparently quite arbitrarily chosen but quite inseparable from its music. I assumed that everyone had this experience and it was a long while before I learned otherwise. In the end I rounded on the images and decided I would use them as a change from letting them wander about my mind uninvited, so I used each scene as the starting point for a poem. I still experience the images, but they have been subjected to a genial exorcism.

One other piece, '107 Poems', had a genesis worth remarking on. Early in his distinguished and dedicated editorship of *Poetry Review*, Eric Mottram, in a moment of acuteness coupled with perversity, suggested I should contribute a longish poem in iambic pentameters, a form I had weaned myself from only with difficulty and resolution. The commission came on a day when I happened to have a hundred and seven images of various sorts by me; so I was able, by setting the pentameters marching off through the heap till it was used up, to respond at least to the perverse element in the invitation.

HANDSWORTH COMPULSIONS

What follows is a revised and extended version of a talk commissioned by Fraser Steel and broadcast on Radio 4 in March 1983. The talk was itself an amplification of the brief explanatory note which accompanied the reprinting of the sequence 'Handsworth Liberties' in my Poems 1955-1980 *(Oxford University Press, 1980).*

Say I'm listening to a jazz record I first heard over forty years ago: 'Home Cooking' by Eddie Condon's orchestra. I've owned copies of it for most of the intervening time. I've played it many times. I know it inside out, and I understand a good deal more about it than I did on the first hearing. I've acquired a copy of the rejected take, with some different musical features. I've seen many photographs of the eight men who made it: I've seen three of them in the flesh and have even worked with one. So this particular three minutes of music, improvised pretty casually one day in 1933 in a New York studio, has been growing up, and growing older, along with me for a long time. Music has changed: I've changed. But as I listen to it I get, quite clearly, the mental image that came into my mind when I first heard it. The image is clear, but unceremonious—after all, it's slipped into its place unbidden and more or less unheeded many times over these last forty years. I called it a mental image. I nearly called it a visual image, but that's not quite what it is. I shall have to try and be more precise. I get the distinct impression that the music is being played on a pleasant sunny morning on the stretch of grass outside what was then Holmes's Garage at the junction of Church Lane and Grove Lane, Handsworth, Birmingham.

By that I don't mean that there are a grand piano and a drum-kit set up by the forecourt, with eight shirtsleeved Americans working away with saxophone, trombone and Prohibition-period liquor jugs, all amid the traffic. I don't see the musicians at all, even though I could picture them easily enough; I don't even visualise their instruments. I just see that little location, an ordinary road junction, familiar to me from early childhood; a place which, as it were, instantly volunteered itself as a home for the sounds which came in through my ears when I first lowered the elephantine pickup of my hand-cranked gramophone on to that Parlophone 78.

I'm thinking of one particular record; but I could tell a similar story for countless items of music that came into my life in my teens. They didn't have to be jazz improvisations, nor was there any class distinction in the various locations my mind allocated to the different sorts of music. 'Spider Crawl', for instance, by Billy Banks and his Rhythmakers, had its existence somewhere in the air of a leafy and peaceful suburban street called Butler's Road, viewed from the north-east. The same patch of roadway, when viewed from the south-west, holds Vaughan Williams's 'Fantasia on a Theme of Thomas Tallis'—or most of it at any rate. Longer works had a tendency to take a walk after a few minutes and pop up again a mile or two away. But tucked up under the branches that used to overhang a long-disappeared set of railings a little way along that same road are the Arietta and its variations from Beethoven's Piano Sonata Opus 111—just as they always have been. The 'Ode to Joy' in the Ninth Symphony provides an exceptional visit to the city centre: it still bursts upon Bull Street, Birmingham, as it looked towards the end of World War II, busy with merrymaking American servicemen on leave, and female war-workers with their brown-painted legs, and dressed in turbans and boxy coats made out of black market army blankets; all milling about among the camouflage-topped buses and the sandbagged department stores. My associative demon must have thought something special was required.

I think my mind started to play this trick only when I reached the age where I started to seek out instrumental music, and to listen to it intensely, even obsessively; at that time my lifelong preference for instrumental over vocal music was decisively formed. Maybe this new experience stimulated my mental imagery into providing something, any old thing, by way of a picture show, in the absence of the quite familiar images I've always had on hearing a vocal performance—I just imagine somebody in the act of singing, maybe in character, maybe not. I always take it for granted, by the way, that everybody has that sort of experience when listening to sung music; but I may be wrong. For it didn't occur to me for many years that my own way of having localities attached to instrumental music wasn't universal. When at last I started asking people whether they recognised the experience, I found nobody at all who did.

So I was left wondering what my peculiarity meant. I have to admit that I think it's of no importance; just a faulty circuit in the brain. It can't be trying to tell me something, or I should surely by now have worked out what the message was. I'm rather more interested in the curious selection of homes my music has been provided with. They aren't places with dramatic, or traumatic, associations. They're not quite 'places' at all. Mostly they are bits of road, seen from a pedestrian's point of view.

Nondescript bits of road, in nondescript weather, suitable for walking. None of them seems to have any particular association or atmosphere. But virtually all of them are, or were, to be found within a mile or two of the house where I spent all my childhood. I had been to other places; I'd seen mountains and rivers and crags and cathedrals and the sea; but what I got issued with to go with my music was some small strip, either of the route between our house and the place a couple of miles off where my maternal grandparents lived, or of the lanes and roadways that led into a patch of lost-looking, left-over, partly-industrialised countryside near our home. Maybe they were both just routes I was used to travelling in a state of reverie, so that the reverie of listening to music just connected itself up with the reverie of walking on familiar ground.

In the mid-seventies I noticed that my poetry was, for a time at least, passing close to these by now long-familiar images, which had up till then seemed too inconsequential to be tackled: mere local coloration, and faint into the bargain. But I was at that time preoccupied with a type of lightly-built poem in which vestigial situations were explored by a kind of uneasy, tentative metaphysic, which sometimes searched for energy and 'meaning' in material of exactly the kind I was using: mental snapshots, taken not because I wanted them but simply because I'd walked through the district year after year with my eyes open and my mind blank. I'd been working with the painter Tom Phillips, and my method had a good deal in common with his characteristic insistence on seeing the backgrounds and marginal details of photographs, postcards and the like, as particularly revealing when brought out of their hiding places and upgraded.

From a list of about thirty scenes I chose sixteen as locales for the poems of 'Handsworth Liberties'—a title which reflects curiosity as to whether my treating the scenes as subjects in their own right would dissolve their bondage to the pieces of music they always accompanied (it didn't). In the poems, I set myself to call up the places as I remembered them at the time of my adolescence and to characterise the tenuous moods they had for me then. To deal with them as they were in 1975 or so was pointless, even though all were still identifiable: dereliction, development and thousands of driving licences, including my own, had by then scattered all the old fields of association and substituted others.

In writing the poems I detached the locations from their musics. That was their liberty, in return for their having to work for me in a new way and earn a little of their keep for a while.

PREFACE TO *A FURNACE*

A Furnace is an engine devised, like a cauldron, or a still, or a blast-furnace, to invoke and assist natural processes of change; to persuade obstinate substances to alter their condition and show relativities which would otherwise remain hidden by their concreteness; its fire is Heraclitean, and will not give off much Gothic smoke.

Some of the substances fed in are very solid indeed: precipitates, not only topographical, of industrial culture in its rapid and heavy onset, when it bred a new kind of city whose images dominated people's intelligences in ways previously unknown.

The poem is also an homage, from a temperament very different from his, to the profound, heterodox and consistent vision of John Cowper Powys, to whom I owe thanks for some words of exhortation he gave me in my youth and in his old age. More importantly, I am indebted to his writings for such understanding as I have of the idea that the making of all kinds of identities is a primary impulse which the cosmos itself has; and that those identities and that impulse can be acknowledged only by some form or other of poetic imagination. There is also, in his novel *Atlantis*, a description of a lost poem which gains its effects by the superimposition of landscape upon landscape rather than rhythm upon rhythm; without having that idea as a scheme I have, indeed, set one landscape to work with another in this poem, more by way of superimposition than comparison: Birmingham, where I was born in a district that had not long since been annexed from the southern edge of the old county of Staffordshire, and the stretch of hill country around the northern tip of the same county where I have been living recently; about the same size as Birmingham, and, in its way, equally complex.

A Furnace is a poem containing a certain amount of history, and the sequence of its movements is based on a form which enacts, for me, the equivocal nature of the ways in which time can be thought about. This is the ancient figure of the double spiral, whose line turns back on itself at the centre and leads out again, against its own incoming curve. After the 'Introit', which identifies the poem's preoccupations in the sort of setting in which they were forcing themselves on me at the time I wrote the pieces which were to be published as *City* in 1961, the seven movements proceed as if by a section taken through the core of such a spiral, with the odd-numbered ones thematically touched by one direction of the spiral's progress, and the even-numbered so touched by its other, returning, aspect; the exception is the fourth section, which is at the centre and thus has the theme of stillness.

1986

Birmingham's What I Think With

Programme Note

Most of Tom Pickard's documentary films have dealt, in a spirit of stubborn, incisive anger rather than nostalgia, with a vanishing subject—the civilization made by working-class people in the industrial North-East. His poems based there brought him to notice in the Sixties; at about that time I was in Birmingham, doing what I could with similar themes, and he and I have known each other's work ever since. Our collaboration was a natural one.

I'm no lyric poet. I'm dedicated to the idea of poetry as a way of understanding what's going on, so the idea of writing a voice-over meditation (published later in my book, *Birmingham River*) was appealing, as was the invitation to record the film's music in the company of some of my favourite players. Appearing on camera was less welcome; but I managed to persuade the battered front door of my birthplace to come out of retirement and stand in for me in many of the shots (it's still leaning against my garage wall, waiting to get paid).

Dodges of this sort (we had trouble, for instance, finding surviving industrial scenes as foul and imposing as those I'd grown up with, and wished we had a budget to shoot in Eastern Europe) along with the compulsively lateral thinking of director and writer, soon combined to dismantle the Day-in-the-Life-of narrative framework we started with. We did stick, though, to our resolve never to have my poetry discussed or explained by talking heads—or even directly illustrated by the visuals—in favour of making it earn its keep by doing a job throughout the film. I'm glad we did so.

REPLY TO PAUL LESTER

I accept the description of the characteristic alienation of the modern poet, compounded by the odd experience of progressively seeing how the work, or the fact of its having been undertaken, is received and handled by the society from which one's already thus alienated. That's familiar to me.

It's not part of your purpose to examine the relationship between "underground" and establishment poetic activity, but it's a question I seem to have raised merely by existing. The two forms of activity seem to me to be demarcated not by a division of substantive issues but behaviourally, by the centripetal effect of a pair of rather turgid whirlpools in different parts of the pond. What distinguishes one from the other is a difference in the conception of how the group and its activities relate, ethically and functionally, to the society. In these terms of allegiance and operation, although I'm obviously much more interested in the actual poetics current in the "underground" group, I don't feel drawn by the gravitational pull of either. For me, to "go underground" and remain there would seem pretentious and academic, just as to "go" in the other direction in the hope of finding a location would seem fatuous. As a result, I get used as a between-worlds counter in reviewers' debates, as in Peter Porter's recent discussion of John Ash's experimentalism, where I'm *the excellent Roy Fisher, whom nobody suggested should be Poet Laureate.*

Paterson is its antecedent in a historical sense to 'City', but not as part of my own experience. I knew of the existence of *Paterson*, but didn't see it until after the period—1957-60—when I was writing the very heterogeneous and unplanned mass of texts from which the 'City' constituents were to be taken. Michael Shayer, who conceived the idea that a live collage might be extracted from the directionless, stranded mass, and who indeed made the selection and arrangement of the 1961 version, *had* read *Paterson*, and no doubt had it in mind. His own long city-poem *Persephone*, based on Worcester (Migrant Press 1962) is well worth reading in this context, and somebody should republish it. And it needs to be said that Michael (a Cambridge-educated scientist and former student of Leavis, deliberately working as a subversive within his own social milieu, as a radical science-master in a public school) had at that time a far more developed set of ideas about the ideological leverage of matters of art than I had.

So the work is a curious collaborative hybrid. The *effect* of the prose/poetry assemblage in 'City' is just as you describe it, and in that respect the comparison with Williams is apt, as is the comment about the way in which both 'Paterson' and 'City' differ from 'The Waste Land'. But the fact remains that the poems used in 'City' were generated in the usual way of single poems, without any thought of subsequent incorporation in a longer work, while the prose pieces had come from another direction.

They'd mostly begin as diary observations, private, not intended for publication, and written with my own *persona*; I'd then started to assemble them into a work called 'The Citizen', which had a romantic and shadowy characterised "I". This is the ghost-text which lies under 'City'. The "I" in it was, it must be said, wholly voyeuristic, alienated, de-politicised and a-social: and the text petered out at the point where, after a couple of hundred pages, I decided I'd better make him have a conversation with another human being. He couldn't get a single word out. So that was the end of him. In *The Ship's Orchestra,* written mainly in 1962, I did a much crisper run-down of this whole matter, by means of taking an "I" character out of the city and sending him to sea—as well as by the use of some actual artistic techniques, which I'd begun to learn about in the interim.

The movement in your commentary from your response to my impressionistic reportage to the detection of the lack of a historical critique is interesting. The impressionism was deliberate, and if those passages work at all, then it's as impressionist pieces, without further analysis adumbrated. It seemed to me most important to record symptoms accurately, before even starting a diagnosis. But not solely visually or photographically, any more than by way of the sort of social data I might have hunted out and used but didn't; I also wanted to include the dimension of affect, the imaginative compulsions of living in the place, as a complete sensory environment. I put that first.

As for the limitation of the technique in penetrating through *the way one sees an ordinary city street* to an understanding of the *means of production,* that's simply answered. I didn't know anything about the means of production. I'd been brought up in the Thirties in a docile working-class environment five doors from an enormous railway-wagon factory which employed, at some time or another, most of the men in the district. My bedroom window looked out into it. But I only once in my life entered it, and that was, ironically, when I was taken in at eight years of age or so to get a distant sight of the King and Queen being shown round it. The assumption of the family and the schools was that children would be, if possible, educated out of the district and of the class, and could then gently cease to concern themselves with all that. What they *would* concern themselves with was left to the dictates of whatever level of the market the elevator let them out at. I didn't meet middle-class socialists until much later, heard no socialism around my street, and can remember only one detectably socialist teacher, who was intriguing but decidedly unworldly. The first time I went into a big factory on a working day was as a twenty-eight-year-old teacher (that was where the elevator had got me to; in fact it had taken me "higher" but I was sulking my way back down through the levels of the meritocracy again) taking my class of backward children round *their* factory—one in which, by another irony, they could never hope to work, since they weren't bright enough.

These aren't offered as excuses; I'm explaining the context of a temperamental naïveté or escapism which is inherent as well as environmental, and which I've had to turn to advantage as best I can. I certainly find it allies me with the aspect of Williams which Pound went for in the 'Dr Williams' Position' essay: a sort of obstinate innocence at best, condemned to a sort of empiricism which is by no means an easy way round problems. I never for a moment bought the vision of stability, prosperity and common purpose which was on offer, much as I would have liked to; I could always see it was riddled with rackets and hypocrisy. But I was stuck with looking at what you call the *street*, the detailed complex product of the generative historical model; I could acknowledge the model, in general terms, but didn't at that time have any appetite for playing with it. (I didn't acquire any useful sense of history until later; and until I had such a sense I couldn't understand how I was myself just such a complex product, like the street, I had the sensation of being free, but of having some impairment—to me unidentifiable—of the intelligence, which made it function ineptly.) I was acquainted for instance with the workshop/factory pattern of Birmingham industry, but didn't then have any sharp sense of those things as means of social and economic manipulation. My father was a workshop employee, a poorly paid craftsman in a small jeweller's in Pitsford Street for most of his life, but he had little to say about it; I do remember that he somehow felt it a penance and socially degrading, when he was moved to a large factory on war work, for three or four times the money.

In the odd quasi-political asides—*the power of will* and so forth, in 'City' I wasn't reaching in towards a critique; I was, in keeping with my programme, staying on the affective surface, of styles of government, aesthetics of persuasion or constraint. And that connects with your response, appropriate I think, to the exaggerated use of language. I was indeed impelled to a certain expressionism of language by what I experienced and the agonised tropes followed naturally enough; and I was, indeed, deliberately fishing, in a prosperous nowhere-city of the Fifties, for the hidden continuation of the hysteria Brecht and Grosz had seen as open and paramount in the early Twenties: I knew there was a streak of it there and I wanted a way of bringing it out. That's the explanation of my choice of that register in preference to something conversational or conventionally post-imagist. 'The Sun Hacks', though, is probably more of a parodic comment an Wordsworth's 'Westminster Bridge' than on nuclear war; and its manner is part of my obsession—which still continues—with the all-pervasiveness of art as the vehicle of thought and so of behaviour, whether it's the décor of a cemetery or the conception of a global political fantasy. I tried, though without, as you say, going out of my way to be explicit, to hit some of that in 'Starting to Make a Tree'. You're not the only reader to assume that the *we* indicates children, so I must have laid—or triggered—a false trail somewhere. For me, they're the men (of course) of an unspecified community, at any time in the history of the race, making themselves at home, building an orientation for themselves as if their particular culture, with its little kit of pragmatism and aesthetics, were the most natural and unquestionable thing in the world. It's one of my rare reveries about the possibility of social order.

Your account of how 'City' isn't a Marxist analysis weighs the matter up well. It follows obviously enough that had I been then possessed of the materials and methods of some sort of Marxist critique, and inclined to use it, I wouldn't have been able to spot the materials of the poem and wouldn't have been forced into some of the lateral metaphoric lurches across the surface which give the thing whatever life it has. The issue is probably more usefully expressed in some such way as the following. I wrote my "surfaces" with the unacknowledged sense of a "real structure" within them, and my understanding of what that structure might be was certainly derived from Marx. But the inclination to display the structure, and thus moralise my observations, wasn't present. For one thing, the alienation had me so powerfully in its grip in my personal life that, like my protagonist in 'The Citizen', I had no word to say about human relationships. For another thing, the thought that I might find myself talking, should I get into print, only to a Marxist audience, more interested in conclusions than in paradoxical evidence, was at odds with my sense of the necessary difficulty of the work.

I have to say that your analysis of the end of 'The Park' is more optimistic than mine. I mean it to say that when the insulting travesty of either rural "Nature" or of gentlemen's quasi-natural gardens, "given" to the public by Victorian manufacturers, philanthropists and municipalities in the form of a public park, has finally descended, with the death of its last bit of swank—the goose—to a vandalised entropic desert of concrete, rubbish and the rest, it's truly come completely into our hands. Big deal! The operative phrase is "If we still want it". In the course of a century or so of that ruthless humbug, pleasure itself has a sour and bewildered taste.

The foregoing remarks about my inability at that period to say anything with confidence about human relationships will no doubt prepare the ground for my saying that I come at the question of reification from the inside, or the further frontiers, rather than from the sane and considerate middle ground. One of the compulsive fantasies of the "I" in *The Citizen* was the wish to becomes gradually, an area at a time, an inscribed black statue, perennial, imperishable and, of course, well out of it all. Not so much in the manner of a reified travesty of a human being, all made up of spare parts like Pynchon's *V* or Poe's *Man Who Was Used Up,* but grandly, more like Senator Yeats contemplating the satisfaction of turning into a metal bird. The only oblique trace of that theme remaining in 'City' is the passage you quote about the statue of the old man in the suburban garden.

So: when the theme of the alarming and surreal qualities of material things, as personality-extensions, prostheses, personality-substitutes, turns up in the 'Interiors', it's an emanation from the writer's progress *towards* the human middle ground en route from a spell of experiencing his own psyche as undergoing petrification. I know that has nothing to do with the way a reader experiences the work, but it may illuminate the way the evaluative strain was arrived at non-programmatically. The programme the work did have was all to do with its varied but repeated images and so on; I wasn't conscious of pursuing a theme at all. Nothing, by the way, is to be assumed about the *Various Figures* of the title. The "I" characters of the individual poems are not meant necessarily to be the same person; and none of them is enacting any scene from the life, to date, of Roy Fisher. Nor are they necessarily male, any or all of them. A few characters such as the shaver, the wrestler, his visitors, have gender, but otherwise it's a matter of the reader's disposition. I did, in fact draft a set of permutations of some of them with the gender-markers reversed as well as a shift from first—to third—person and so on (e.g. *Why should she let me shave the hairs from her body?* etc) but the effect was merely camp, and it diffused the sense of confinement that was part of the design. For it's the rooms, those environing objects, that are the prime realities, and the personages are their emanations.

That theme of an oppressive material world, confronting the senses and generating a metaphysic of unease and madness, was present in the 'Five Morning Poems' of 1959, and appeared again in the 'Interiors', 'Seven Attempted Moves', and *The Ship's Orchestra* of the early Sixties. All of these enact attempts desperate or comic, to dissolve a sense of oppressive solidity, an impenetrable stasis, in all phenomena—not just bourgeois possessions or urban scenery. By 1965 or so, the stasis—brought on, as you might well say, by prolonged addiction to the study of appearances and end-products without the saving presence or some overriding and mobilising principle—was in full possession and endured a block which lasted four or five years.

The writings of the years following the block—'The Cut Pages', 'Matrix', 'Handsworth Liberties' and many of the short poems which deal with conundrums of perception or of artistic rendering, photography and so forth—are thus much concerned with processes of loosening, slackening and psychic mobility and relativity, much as one pokes and worries at a knot that's been pulled too tight and has fused into an unyielding, solid structure. That is why the ostensible subject-matter of those poems is so often art, and the perception of images. I was in there hunting for the enemy, the demon of fixity and solidity.

The openness of my preferred forms is thus partly a matter of my own imaginative self-preservation as well as being, as you rightly say, in some sense an expression of a political attitude.

'107 Poems' is an oddity, rather than a tendency, and not too much should be inferred from it. I should perhaps have either explained or dropped it. It's the response to a (partly) flippant suggestion from Eric Mottram in the days of his editorship of *Poetry Review* that I should write him a longish run of iambic pentameters. I chose to use, along with the steadily-beating form, a chance or cut-up method of producing images. That's all. The sort of thing that doesn't puzzle people too much in painting or music.

I've had to assume, since this debate between observation and social interpretation has been so central to my work, has lasted so long and has been so productive of strenuous intellectual discomforts in me, that my handling of it is, in some sense, my theme and not just my biography. That is, I see myself as having been educated, culturally destined if you like, by my class, temperament and timing, to point myself into what you call "problems" which I was equipped to see, but not to see round. I developed a quite daunting vision of the world, which by its very particularity, challenged me to find a way of dissolving it.

It seems to me now that in such work as I've done fairly recently—'Wonders of Obligation', written in 1979, various shorter pieces done since then, and particularly the long poem 'A Furnace'—I have, for good or ill, turned the matter inside-out and have access to an "I" which I don't have to characterise or play games with; and thus to a pretty direct and discursive approach to a heterogeneous array of material which interests me and comes under my hand as I want it to; that is, it doesn't just squat across my path. I have to admit, rather uneasily, that I may just be at the mercy of my original material, and that my sense of mental liberation comes only as consequence of the real dismantling of the industrial base, and a good deal of the physical presence, of the urban Midlands.

INSIDE A VARIOUS ART:
SOME OF THE WAYS POEMS ARE MADE

Every human language I've ever heard of has poetry as one of its dialects. In saying that I know that, temporarily, I'm misusing the term "dialect", when it might seem more proper to say "register"—that is to say the particular transaction the language is engaged in: a sermon, a pub conversation, a Last Will and Testament, an attempt to persuade the public to support your decision to declare war, a love letter. I shall have more to say about register later; but for the moment I'll say merely that the catalogue of registers available to language-uses that could be recognised as poetic is so vast and so open-ended, ranging from epics through genealogical tables to jokes and epigrams, as to make the term useless as a description. I make a glancing use of the word dialect as a means of stressing the singularity of poetry in a culture and its language: the way dialects of region or class withdraw and consolidate themselves, for the culture to use or neglect as it sees fit.

So much for attempts to generalise. You can see the perils in the way my words have to spend so much of their time covering their retreat. What I shall now do is to try to recapture as much as I can of the way I came by a number of my poems and of the things I found myself taking into consideration as I made them. They are thirty or forty years old, well beyond the reach of my wondering whether I ought to have made them differently, and they are also congealed by repeated publication. I've written a good deal about this city, where I was born and spent nearly all of my first forty-odd years: so in recognition of that fact and of many significant associations with this building, this Institute and its former home on the corner of Paradise Street and Ratcliff Place—and even the Education Office across the street—I've chosen pieces with many local references.

The first is a straightforward social piece but it raises the question of register on several levels. Here's the situation. It's 1971. A well-established magazine that often prints my poems asks for something new. Although a literary magazine without overt political content or commentary pages it has impeccable socialist credentials and an anti-elitist policy. Nevertheless, since it carries only stories, poems and reviews and demands a certain level of craft, its readership is *de facto* restricted almost entirely to people whose education has left them feeling at ease with that sort of material. As I consider the sort of poem I might write that paradox hangs in my mind. I go back to 1957, when I was trying to teach a class of forty-seven children, the lowest stream of the top year of what would nowadays be called a sink junior school on the remote eastern edge of Birmingham: a spacious dystopian estate where the population of the inner-city Garrison Lane area had been rehoused a generation earlier. I decide to make a poem of the paradox, using that memory, and designed specifically for that magazine. I call the poem 'One World':

One World

When I last saw them they were eleven
born on a council estate
halfway to the next town,
sold into the lowest stream
at five or so: you can recognise
a century of Brummagem eugenics
in a child. It was a school
where three out of a hundred
passed for Selective forms
in a worker-zone Comprehensive.
But not these. It was late:
apart from their other troubles
they couldn't read.

I was no help. Most days
they scared hell out of me: I taught
pacification and how to play.
I lived for the moment and trusted nothing.

By now some are dead. I read of one
suicide and one broken skull.
The rest will be going on thirty. About them
I know I can generalise without offence.
But to name names: if John Snook,
Ann Pouney or Brian Davidson,
Pat Aston or Royston Williams
should of their own accord and unprompted
read over this and remember me—well
if they're offended they can tell me about it.
It would be good to know
we all look at the same magazines.

I heard nothing, of course. And not one of those children, who will now be in their late fifties, subscribes to *Friends Reunited*. I've looked. It was probably some of them who, when they graduated to the secondary school on the site, virtually destroyed the neighbouring railway station and forced it to close.

You've heard the poem's origin. I can say something about how the writing of it went. There was no difficulty about the tone: I like to use language that lies close to ordinary conversation—to *my* conversation at any rate—and what I had to tell called for no special effects of weather, lighting or poetic rumblings. And I knew from the first roughly how long the poem would need to be and how its lines could simply fall, with an actual avoidance of rhythmic symmetry. So in one sense it really was just a matter of writing the thing down. But there was the familiar spectre of exposition barring the entry to the poem. Exposition's a skill most writers have to acquire: novelists—"typists" I call them when I'm feeling jealous—historians, journalists. Poets do have ways of getting off lightly; but it can be a chore, and it tends to delay movement, something which is as crucial in a poem as it would be in a piece of music. I had the comparatively simple task of rattling off a bunch of familiar social observations (though at that time there was far less public coverage of such things), with a built-in slant, and in the shortest possible space. I did all I could in nine short lines.

There was a little tuning to do. Should I call it 'One World' or 'One Nation' as in the sense of 'One-nation Conservatism' or even 'One-nation Socialism?' I decided the second option would look too pointed without actually pointing anywhere. Again, should I say "it would be good to know we all look at the same magazines" or "it would be nice to know"? It seemed to me that "good to know" somehow smuggled in "nice to know" without tying a little bow on it. It's a one-idea poem and my work was simply to set the idea up so that it would run easily.

To say a little more about the business of setting a scene or a situation, particularly one taken from life: often the writer will have an instant grasp of the whole thing, packaged like a closed hand. Then it has to be prised open a little way so that the minimum of suggestive details can be lifted out for the quickest delivery possible. I've described writing, particularly poetry, as "blind fishing in the association-fields of people you're not likely ever to meet." That's all the control a writer can expect to exercise. When I was working with schoolchildren and student teachers I used to set an exercise on the lines of the work a famous teacher, Marian Richardson, had developed quite early in the last century at the College of Art in this very street. The group, with closed eyes, would be given an extremely brief instruction, such as imagining opening an unfamiliar door and looking into a previously unseen room; or, conversely, opening an unfamiliar door and looking out at a previously unseen street or landscape, then reporting what appeared to the inner eye. The individual reports were always so varied as to be surprising and entertaining, though the exercise itself was simple enough: all I had to do was take care not to elaborate or suggest; and in particular not to prolong the instruction in such a way as to confuse the mental experience I suspected everyone had already formed instantly.

What was anything but simple was what followed. Most people would have reported, often in detail, what met their eyes: what was in focus. Then a few questions from me would demonstrate that for many of them such tacit, unexamined presences as the time of day, the season, what lay behind the observer, the weather, the general narrative mood were recoverable from where they lay packed in the original response. That's where the blind fishing goes on.

The next piece I want to look at had its very local origin in a few moments' observation no more than two or three hundred yards from where we are now. I call it 'Magritte Imitated Himself', and though it's again short this one has several layers of ideas, which presented themselves very rapidly and then had to be sorted so as to be fed into the poem. René Magritte was a straight-faced, literalist illustrator of bizarre notions, some of which lie close enough to the way many of us sometimes privately look at the world to ensure his popularity. And when he ran short of ideas he would copy his own work and sell it one more time. The visual joke that chimed immediately with the experience in the poem was the one where a window looks out on a frozen mountainous landscape. One pane is broken and lies fallen against the wall: it still bears the image it will have had before. But so also does the hole it left.

Magritte Imitated Himself

I looked out of the window
once too often
(you'll stick like it)
and on a cold Sunday

afternoon of the Seventies
in Birmingham
stood for the first time, disaffected,
on the aerial concrete
approach-platform of the new
Library, reared over the ghosts
of Widman and Dodd, Civil
Military and Ecclesiastical
Tailors, and Mason College, the old
Arts building. Glancing to one side
I saw a skyline of certain
venerable cornices
in form of a frameless window
printed on the world.

Lost window, persistent world:
the place where I stood in the wind
was a sort of same; the space
where my customary seat in the first-floor
English Theatre used to be. They had
torn down all my support, removing
the very street beneath, then
raised it somehow up again, that
my attention could once more
wander. Starlings
used sometimes to fly about during lectures
and would look
ill-at-ease, time-travelling.

My poems of distant travel now have to shuffle a few steps to the area
between the Council House and the Town Hall. Forty years ago this was
a smaller, cluttered space with traffic on three sides of it and no wide fan
of steps. It was a quite interesting repository of heterogeneous Victorian
monuments and statuary. My poem is mistitled, through an oversight
of my own, 'The Memorial Fountain'. I had forgotten that it was in his
lifetime that Joseph Chamberlain had indulged his fancy for erect tributes
to himself, even requiring the red-brick Ottoman campus of the University
at Edgbaston to be completed by a clock tower copied from the one in
the Piazza San Marco in Venice. The poem, though, is not historical. It

concerns appearances and aesthetics. Just forty years ago last month I'd been reading Donald Davie's *Ezra Pound: the Poet as Sculptor* and had been interested in Davie's emphasis on the way in which Pound, when not being diffuse and didactic, had made great efforts to make his images seem as durable as they would have been if carved. On a summer Sunday evening I took a drive into the city centre, trying, in a way, to see familiar scenes as I imagined Pound might have seen them. I knew I'd find nothing of the classical Mediterranean culture Pound often favoured; but even so I was taken aback by what I did see. Birmingham was being visited by a sunset so lurid and vulgar that only a very bad painter could have done it justice. Yet, leaving the architecture out of it, the blue enamel sky decorated with shiny orange clouds was not man-made: it was Nature, the benchmark of art since the Romantics. I had something to think about there.

And at the same time I wanted to "do" it if I could; and as the sunset faded the scene began to look manageable. I stared at it, captured it, and within a day or so wrote my poem, starting with care for detail, then letting it take me where it seemed to want to go. As you'll hear, it didn't after all take me in the direction of a debate on the vulgarity of Nature: instead it required me to make a self-portrait of my own detachment.

The Memorial Fountain

The fountain plays
                    through summer dusk in gaunt shadows,
black constructions
                    against a late clear sky,
water in the basin
                    where the column falls
        shaking,
rapid and wild,
                    in cross-waves, in back-waves,
        the light glinting and blue,
as in a wind
                    though there is none.
                            Harsh
skyline!
              Far-off scaffolding
bitten against the air.

                    Sombre mood
in the presence of things,
                no matter what things;
respectful sepia.

        This scene:
        people on the public seats
        embedded in it, darkening
        intelligences of what's visible;
        private, given over, all of them –

Many scenes.

Still sombre.

As for the fountain:
                nothing in the describing
beyond what shows
            for anyone;
        above all
no "atmosphere".
                It's like this often –
I don't exaggerate.

        And the scene?
        A thirty-five-year-old man,
        poet,
                by temper, realist,
        watching a fountain
        and the figures round it
        in garish twilight,
                    working
        to distinguish an event
        from an opinion;
                    this man,
        intent and comfortable—

Romantic notion.

I'd not been expecting to be taken off at a tangent in that way; but perhaps I should have foreseen something of the kind, for it's a shape quite a number of my poems have come to follow. Two issues need looking at in fact. One is the idea, familiar from the accounts of many writers, painters and musicians: that the work in hand seems to have a life of its own and proceeds independently of the creator—characters in a novel take over and speak and move for themselves and so forth. I'd limit it to a sense that, once conceived and however vaguely, the poem knows best and had better not be pushed and prodded along. As with exposition I attribute that to the apparently instantaneous arrival of a package of ideas that can be unpacked with due care later.

The other issue has to do with symmetry. Very many works of art, of whatever kind, are structured so as to arrive at finality, preferably well-earned. I can think of poems that haven't earned their conclusions and seem to need Q.E.D. added: sometimes they wag their tails. I've nothing against poems that know their whole course: I merely know that I'm so tidy-minded by nature that I tend to overdo the moment of tucking-up. So I make a virtue of escapism, knowing that my escape route may well lead me to somewhere challenging or uncomfortable. Here's another poem that has a local starting point but which in the writing took me into a world of mutability and dream. The movement of the poem is somnolent and comfortable, and it ends so: but the environment towards the close is far less stable than the one at the beginning—which is, should you know it, Edgbaston reservoir. Again it's a summer evening forty years ago.

After Working

> I like being tired,
> to go downhill from waking
> late in the day
> when the clay hours
> have mostly crossed the town
> and sails smack on the reservoir
> bright and cold;
>
> I squat there by the reeds
> in dusty grass near earth
> stamped to a zoo patch
> fed with dog-dung

and where swifts
flick sooty feathers along the water
agape for flies.

The thoughts I'm used to meeting
at head-height when I walk or drive
get lost here in the petrol haze
that calms the elm tops
over the sunset shadows I sit among;

and I watch the sails,
the brick dam,
the far buildings brighten,
pulled into light,
sharp edges and transient,
painful to see:

signal to leave looking and
shaded, to fall away
lower than dulled water reaches,
still breathing the dog odour
of water, new flats, suburb trees,
into the half light of a night garage
without a floor,

then down its concrete stems
shaded as I go down
past slack and soundless
shores of what might be other
scummed waters
to oil-marked asphalt
and, in the darkness, to a sort of grass.

The Birmingham poems I've picked out for this evening's purposes have all
been short and self-sufficient for obvious reasons. But it would be wrong
to suppose that my imaginative interest in the locality chiefly takes the
form of staring at bits of it and proceeding to puzzle over what I see. It
has been something much wider and more pervasive. The Arts Council

film I made with Tom Pickard some years ago took a casual remark of mine as a title: *Birmingham's What I Think With*; and that holds good even though I've not lived in the city for many years. For my earliest, and developing, impressions of the world—its physical presence, authorities, human character and behaviour and the mandates by which we lived, died and were buried—were laid down within a very small area. And with age—and what we're told about the poor durability of recent memory as against the clarity and sudden recovery of quite remote memories is true—I'm often back in my birthplace reliving learning experiences I had not long after infancy, that period when the exploring senses are alert but the brain has not yet developed its filing system of classes and categories that enables information to be assessed and stored without its having first to be sniffed, touched or sucked.

In the late 1950s, after a few years away, I returned to Birmingham and found that early curiosity reviving in me, or at least in part of my life, and it led me to publish, with a certain amount of unease, a collage of poetry and prose which I called 'City' in which I was virtually the only character, the only inhabitant. I *did* know there were a million or so other people about. I had a family; I spent my working days with dozens of student teachers, often darting at speed from one busy or beleaguered school to another; I spent several evenings a week playing the piano in heaving jazz clubs or in Soho Road shebeens where I sometimes seemed the token white in a black band; I was on a committee that was making an early attempt at smoothing racial integration. But the revived curiosity that produced the work called 'City' was in a sector of my mind that hadn't altogether grown up. I didn't do the grown-up thing and study the city's industrial history or its economics or its sociology or even its civic administration. I had a compulsion to experience its aesthetic impact: I would take long, unstructured solitary walks or bus-rides at odd hours to wherever the destination boards said. The only rule was that there was to be no actual business for me to transact when I got there. I took my guidance from William Blake: "What is now real was once only imagin'd", and also the politics of what I was about. It was evident that virtually every scrap of the enormous body of the place was the product, for good or ill, of a human brain. I was simply an observer, looking at what ideas had managed to bring about. I still think we ought to know all we can about how ideas happen.

So it was an inward, ingested city, distinct from the one I lived and worked in and interacted with, that I wrote about at that time. I didn't even name it, so that anybody who might read my work wouldn't be automatically entitled to have the automatic dismissive reactions that mentions of Birmingham can still trigger.

In the last poem I'll talk about the local material is nowhere near the surface until it's brought out by an access of involuntary memory. I spent many years working whenever I could as a jazz club pianist. And I was sitting at home alone, miles from Birmingham, doing what I would call practising. If you regularly play improvised, unscored music, particularly in the company of other musicians, you are, on however lowly a level, composing as you go. And part of your preparation needs to consist of trying out the resources of your own instrument so that you know how this or that voicing or timbre is likely to work when the moment calls for it. Accordingly, I was, as the poem says, clanging along in A flat, devising patterns of fourths and fifths: these are intervals that can in fact clang metallically, particularly in the middle register of the piano. I'm used to being carried to places, sometimes remembered, sometimes imagined, when I listen to other people's music. But as I played I realised that the quite harsh sound of my own inventions was dumping me back in Kentish Road, Handsworth, at the age of about four, surrounded by the sounds and images of the nearby railway and the factory line that ran by the end of the garden. And it produced the somehow related figure of Granny Timms from two doors up, long gone and utterly forgotten. I can't say any part of this memory-flood pleased me particularly; but its workings certainly intrigued me.

There's one note I should give. In the phrase "thinking of Mary Lou" Mary Lou is Mary Lou Williams, a widely respected black pianist whose career stretched from about 1930 to about 1980. She wasn't a showy player, but she had a proverbially authoritative way of realising ideas on the keyboard and a touch to match. I called the poem 'The Home Pianist's Companion', a title that's meant to suggest a manual of useful exercises but is also a reminder that when you believe you're alone with your piano you're not. Your mind is with you and you can have no idea what it will get up to.

If you can follow me through this little maze I can promise you you'll be free when you reach the exit.

The Home Pianist's Companion

Clanging along in A-flat
correcting faults,

minding the fifths
and fourths in both hands
and for once
letting the tenths look out
for their own chances,

thinking of Mary Lou,
a lesson to us all,

how she will trench and
trench into the firmness of the music
modestly;

thinking,
in my disorder of twofold sense,
or finding rather
an order thinking for me as I play,
of the look of lean-spoked
railway wagon wheels
clanging on a girder bridge,
chopping the daylight, black
wheel across wheel, spoke

over rim, in behind girder and out
revealing the light, withholding it,
inexorable flickers
of segments in overlap
moving in mean elongate
proportions, the consecutive
fourths of appearances,
harsh gaps, small strong
leverages, never still.

The sour face
on that kind of wheel:

I've known that
ever since I first knew anything;
a primary fact of feeling,
of knowing how
best to look after yourself.

Clanging along in A-flat, and
here they come,
the apports, the arrivals:
fourths, wheel-spokes,
and rapidly the eternal
mask of a narrow-faced cat,
its cornered, cringing intensity
driving me to distraction again.

But into the calm
of a time just after infancy
when most things were still
acceptable

this backward image-trail
projects further
on a straight alignment
across what looked to be emptiness,
checked as void

and suddenly locates the dead,
the utterly forgotten:

primal figure of the line,
primitively remembered,
just a posture of her, an apron,
a gait. Vestigial figure,
neighbouring old woman
gaunt, narrow-faced, closed-in,
acceptable,
soon dead.

Still in the air
haunting the fourths

of A-flat major
with wheels and a glinting cat-face;

reminding me
what it was like to be sure,
before language ever
taught me they were different,
of how some things were the same.

Roy Fisher on Roy Fisher

When Roy Fisher was lying paralysed in hospital for much of last year, unable to do more than collaborate distantly with Andrew McAllister of Bloodaxe on the preparation of *The Dow Low Drop*, he bound himself, so it's said, by a great oath: to refrain from writing any book of poems about lying paralysed in hospital. "Why should I become rich and famous?" he'd say. If this story is true, it illustrates and exposes the sustained diffidence of the man once referred to by Peter Porter as "the excellent Roy Fisher, whom no one suggested should be made Poet Laureate". Given profitable copy by a malign fate, it was quite in character for Fisher, selflessly or through arrogance, to leave the field clear for similarly afflicted people of the sort who write in the broadsheets. As for the Laureateship, he was among those who—at its change of tenant in 1984—were recommending its abolition on the grounds that it brought the art into disrepute and ridicule.

An approving review of one of Fisher's early books wrote: "Insofar as Fisher can be said to have a subject… it has to be the Provinces." In the face of a welcome like that, Fisher can probably be forgiven for going instantly to ground and conducting the remainder of his public career from various positions of concealment, his manoeuvrings occasionally revealed as he moves from one patch of cover to another. The elusiveness probably had a much longer history. In his essay in the *Contemporary Authors Autobiography Series* (reprinted in this volume as 'Antebiography') he tells how for years in his tough Birmingham primary school he kept himself in one piece only by being "The Daft Kid", too much of an idiot to be fun to beat up, though all the while surreptitiously coming top in schoolwork. Open self-assertion and proselytising conviction seem to be faculties he was born without, and his merits as a writer come by a different route: although he's not personally reclusive it's impossible to imagine Fisher ever burning to set up a reading-series, issue a manifesto, edit a magazine or a didactic anthology, or solicit an opportunity to barnstorm schoolchildren into admiring his meticulous, low-key accounts of Breton ossuaries. His work appears to have come about almost entirely in response to outside initiatives. He habitually publishes, and, one suspects, even writes, only when pressed, as if feeling a need to keep his flying hours up and his accreditation open.

LATE STARTER

He was a late starter in any case. He was over thirty before his first pamphlet, *City*, appeared and a further six years passed before there was a book, *The Ship's Orchestra*, by which time he was well into a writer's block, which was to last him until 1970, its end coinciding with his emergence from an intermittently haunted and phobic period of his life. All the same, Fisher has now been on the scene for a long while. By various shifts and dedicated efforts his writings have been progressively collected and kept in print almost without lapse for thirty-five years. Even so, it apparently hasn't always been easy for people to get a clear view of what he's been up to. From the first there's been a tendency to sideline him as being probably somebody else's baby. For years he was described as having his reputation-needs taken care of by Americans; or he was a painter masquerading as a writer; or a jazz musician straying into words and out again. The *TLS* review of his 1980 interim *Collected* appeared in print shorn by editorial cartography of the reviewer's original assumption that the work existed in the same world—heterodox enough, you might think—as that of the Faber Four of the time, Larkin, Gunn, Hughes, Heaney (none of them, incidentally, appreciably greedier for celebrity than Fisher). The map left him, as before, in charge of his own off-shore island in the middle of England, hung in deep international space somewhere off Spaghetti Junction. In recent years the style has been to commend him warmly and for the right reasons, while remarking on his inexplicable neglect—"an offence against public decency" as *Bête Noire* grandly called it.

The Dow Low Drop—the title's taken from a still-fragmentary long sequence based on a monstrous quarry-scar near his home—is in the main a very substantial Selected which makes the greater part of his work available again, more clearly and approachably arranged than previously. The selection includes, uncut, the sequences 'City', 'Wonders of Obligation', 'It Follows That', 'Metamorphoses', and the fictional (one hopes) 'Interiors With Various Figures' and also two complete books: *The Ship's Orchestra* and *A Furnace*; the latter, for all its unconscious or unashamed solipsism, one of the most ambitious recent English poems I've read. These works take up, as they should, almost two thirds of the book, and the fact illustrates something consistent in Fisher's approach. With no gift for the anecdotal-discursive, self-contained, teachable A4 poem, he's happiest at the extremes of duration: the three-or-four-line fragment or the forty-page long haul, And this takes us to the heart of what he's about. I think he's a Romantic, gutted and kippered by two centuries' hard knocks. The willingness to regard his sketch-books as exhibitable ('Diversions', 'It Follows That') and to go on shamanic mental trips though humdrum-looking material are the indicators. Either way, the technique is one of epiphanic revelation. He doesn't judge his material; he lets it judge him, in the form of his ability to perceive and render it. If he can't see anything he can't say anything. There's a considerable and, I should guess, carefully-preserved naïveté at work here.

LACONIC ENDINGS

This watch-and-wait approach probably gives a better explanation of his disinclination to predict the course of a poem or to structure perorations than does the usual one that it's something brought across from his work as a jazz musician. The jazz link is most likely a matter of style and tone, in that he's a poet of insidious openings, occasional sustained flights and laconic endings, signs which mark a few genres of jazz music rather than the radical theory of instant improvisation, which isn't, of course, peculiar to jazz. And other forms of music have their place in the poetry: in a radio interview, for instance, Fisher once described the contribution Shostakovich's flayed clarity had made to his treatment of the dead in 'A Furnace'.

Fisher's an effective phrase-maker, and he'd be eminently quotable, if only anybody could find a reason to quote him. The tone is habitually exact and unexcited, and he's obviously a writer who tugs the seams of his syntax to see if they hold. (The satires are exceptions: there the material's slung down happily just as it comes, and is the better for it.) Mostly he makes little distinction between verse and prose—one of his favourite line-forms is in fact a series of very short prose paragraphs—and he moves with equal ease in both. By contrast, the very few examples of his critical prose and reviewing to reach print show signs of struggle. Given a subject to address, he grows adjectival and simile-ridden, with dependent clauses cramming themselves into the sentences wherever they can, like piglet runts scrambling to find an unsucked dug. He clearly prefers freedom.

ABSTEMIOUS

Occasionally in the poems, though, he'll let himself get trapped, almost as if on purpose, into a corner where the only way out is by using one of the grand abstractions. At such points he's capable of turning on the poor word as if resentfully, treating it as opaque, a stray item from other people's language. There's a curious parallel here with the jazz pianist Joe Sullivan, with whose intensely emotional and declamatory playing Fisher admits to having been obsessed since boyhood. Sullivan, alcoholic and of uncertain temper, would sometimes impatiently belabour his own music, often by spastic repetitions, as if frustrated by the limitations of his medium. He's an interesting allegiance in any case for the notoriously emollient and abstemious Fisher, on whom the considered verdict of the Contained Cambridge School, sent across country by messenger some days after he'd first read there, ran: "He only drank a pint and a half all night". The same town brought out the emollience, too: it's recorded that when the organisers of the Cambridge Poetry Festival invited participants to list others with whom they wouldn't appear, Fisher was the only one to send in a nil return. There are, indeed, grounds for suspecting that Fisher has never learned enough about his fellow poets to understand why he should dislike them. (Certainly he's always been happier to be out fighting the jazz club pianos of his beloved Provinces.)

Several commentators have noted uneasily that the list of things Fisher's poetry omits to mention has to include social optimism; and that omission, combined with his willingness to invoke and inspect images of awe, pomp and intimidation, leads them into wondering whether there isn't maybe a covert political nostalgia for that sort of thing. The evidence all points the other way. Fisher's political disposition is plain enough to see: it constantly breaks the surface of 'A Furnace', though never programmatically and is generally apparent once recognised. Nostalgia has no part in it. I take him to be an anarchist who simply has no time whatever for hierarchical systems, monotheisms or state authority; or for capitalism, along with the absorbent, malleable selves it breeds and with which it populates its democracies and its literatures. For Fisher the world ruled by such rackets is nevertheless the only world, into which everybody's born already swimming or going under. He's about as right-wing as Luis Buñuel.

From Fisher's previously collected work this *New and Selected* omits half a dozen sizeable sequences, some lesser ones and sixty or seventy single poems, as well as the extended prose work *The Cut Pages* from 1971 (republished jointly in 1985 by Oasis and Shearsman) and the 1994 collection *Birmingham River*. So there's a volume of some weight in prospect when all these texts are gathered together. Your reviewer, for one, hopes that book won't be so long delayed as to be a Posthumous Collected.

III

On Poets and Others

Death by Adjectives

Being a response in the form of a review to the gift of the
millennial reissue of Columbia's Piano Moods *albums.*

Piano Moods is a dated title, dragged forward fifty years, and there's plenty of genuine historical interest to be found in George Avakian's account of the early evolution of the microgroove compilation and in the work of the twelve pianists then enlisted, with others, to service its needs. The pianist Dick Katz's essay gives an expert, sometimes tolerant, view of what goes on. The original idea was to set up montages of continuous piano playing and there's a good deal of obliging amenity-music here, by pianists no longer much heard. But some of the work, and the most valuable, doesn't fit the uniform, which gets ripped apart. The sets by Hines, Sullivan and Wilson are important jazz records and always have been: the Tatum concert is still a towering masterpiece.

Earl Hines's ways of opening the music out and knocking it right along always seem to me more consistently audacious than his once-celebrated gambles with time and phrasing. When the tracks by Hines were first issued as 78s and on LP they were said to show the great innovator of the twenties in the placidity of middle age. Huh. There's little rest for the listener here, and no somnambulism by the pianist. He lets Al McKibbon's bass and the wonderful stealthy drumming of J. C. Heard, the sound of 42nd Street in the forties, vamp for him while he goes wherever he wants. There's nothing in jazz like the romping up-tempo passages in *You Can Depend on Me* and *I Hadn't Anyone Till You*, where he lopes relentlessly away with the left while grabbing jagged, sidelong treble phrases apparently out of nowhere. In fact they're out of the pretty plain harmonic progressions, but by no route anybody could have foreseen. This is why intelligent musicians took to playing jazz.

Teddy Wilson, by catching the spirit of what the horn players were moving into, wrote almost the whole working vocabulary of swing piano, opening it up to virtually everybody in the business and seeing it carried on right through bop by Hank Jones and Tommy Flanagan, and all the pianists who favoured open lines: a whole long generation. At his peak between the mid-thirties and mid-forties, he's caught here still in splendid form, before the setting in of the gradual, gentle, apparently painless decline which saw his music lose its edge of timing and structure: its jazz, in short.

Jess Stacy's regarded with considerable affection by followers of the swing bands and small Dixieland groups he played with, and this is somewhat surprising, since his austere, purposeful playing, with its steely touch and introspective bass lines, can be quite forbidding. Rarely an ingratiating melodist, he goes for direct drive, with an unparalleled sense of lift. He was at his best when responding to a band, climbing his way up from under and dominating the proceedings without using cheap tricks. Left to himself without that challenge, he was sometimes liable to wander rather than develop, and the solos here, taken from a number of sessions with a very crisp Hollywood rhythm section, make good listening without often reaching classic status. One memorable oddity is what must be the briskest version of Beiderbecke's *In a Mist* ever recorded.

Ralph Sutton, though not always audibly kind to pianos, is kind to tunes, often venerable and neglected ones: a gentleman escort who could give these old ladies a good time to the point of breathlessness but without lasting physical damage. His numbers tend to be springy workouts, with only rare improvisatory surprises. I've heard a more inventive and intricate American pianist refer to him ironically as 'Ralph Subtle', and he was never an imaginative or emotional heavyweight, but you certainly hear a piano getting thoroughly played, and with two large hands. And for all the gung-ho, he's no thug: these are harmonically sound and balanced keyboard arrangements.

The selection of Fats Waller's fragmentary, back-of-envelope sketches posthumously worked up to performing level, with some lacunae filled, by his friend Joe Sullivan provide no opportunity for the magnificent brooding that often characterised Sullivan's playing. Even Fats' most successful tunes tend to be catchy bat-and-ball sets of two-bar (or, as in *Ain't Misbehavin'* and *Honeysuckle Rose*, one-bar) phrases, and some of these scraps, like *What's Your Name?*, are made from only the most basic of musical materials. But *There'll Come a Time When You'll Need Me* is a serviceable standard, and *Breezin'* is a pretty finger-routine tune Willie the Lion Smith could have written. Maybe he did, one night. Other piano players like to play this one. Sullivan makes no gesture towards Fats' engaging pneumatic bounce, but does all of it his own declamatory way, with a ringing, conclusive account of each number, accompanied by bass and the happy drumming of the like-minded George Wettling. The vigour displayed is sometimes astonishing, particularly in the up-tempo ride-outs, where he smashes on through with (fortunately) an air of complete conviction. If Hines at one time played Armstrong on the piano, Sullivan, as well as being the John Ford of the piano, is Wild Bill Davison and all his Commodores.

I've always been interested in tracking down the under-recorded musicians who stayed around Chicago after the Goodman-Krupa-Freeman-Stacy-Spanier-Wettling-Tough wave had moved out to the swing bands and Eddie Condon's New York circle: one of them was Max Miller, sometimes praised but elusive on record. Hearing him at last I was disappointed. His set runs to rather heavy, tricksy pianistics: these aren't nice ideas. From occasional passages I get a sense that under the show, or ten years back from it, there are the remains of a useful Chicago-Dixieland player like Floyd Bean or Tut Soper, but that wasn't what he was about in this context.

Miller was primarily a commercial studio pianist, as were Buddy Weed, Stan Freeman and Bill Clifton. The occupational hazard of studio musicians is that although they stay clear of dud venues, get paid and keep in wonderful technical shape, they spend their lives actually listening to the garbage they play, and it gets into the bloodstream. Weed plays deftly and agreeably, but it's background music foregrounded, and the patterns on the wallpaper get obtrusive. Clifton, though, is a find, a splendid executant who deals out good standard tunes with an obvious care for piano sound and a contained sense of taste. He reaches for the idiom of the time — easy bebop, Shearing — and doesn't do anything very original, but had he spent longer in the public eye with the Goodman and Herman bands he would certainly have attracted a following. The band-leader Eddie Heywood can be studied with this group. An accomplished pianist of great fluency, he has an incisive touch (beautifully recorded here, as are most of the sets) to rival Tatum's or Nat Cole's, making you think he's about to play jazz—only he never does.

Stan Freeman plays jazz quite often during his eight numbers, but does some terrible things in between. This set's instructive in the light it throws back on the temptations facing keyboard players in the days before synthesizers took over the temptation business and ran with it. In fact, the old hazards bear a great similarity to what's now behind the coloured preset programme buttons on a big home synthesizer—Latin, Classical, Country and Western, Hip Hop, Bossa Nova, Kletzmer, Jazz. "Jazz" is an effect you can turn on for half a chorus and drop. This is what Freeman, in what sounds like a wholly scored trio showcase set, does. He has fantastic technique and a masterful musical intelligence, and much of the music is well worth attention. But not for long at a stretch. He goes off into waltzes, bits of Boccherini and stretches of Old Music Master twaddle, glitteringly played. The whole thing sounds like a piano company product-demonstration sampler.

In the early fifties Erroll Garner, Ahmad Jamal and Joe Bushkin (already a youthful veteran of the bands of Berigan, Goodman and Tommy Dorsey) were doing the prudent thing and making themselves popular. In an outwardly smooth era, brand-identity and packaging held the keys, with residencies, concert tours and Songbook albums taking the place of ballroom one-nighters, juke-box singles and jam sessions. It was a time of high-class novelties—the Gerry Mulligan Quartet, the Dave Brubeck Quartet, J and K, the MJQ, the Chico Hamilton Quintet—mostly in the tradition of Artie Shaw's restless innovations of a generation earlier. The solo pianists didn't lean so much towards classical ideas, but they tended to stress their marketable idiosyncrasies. Garner's set is bright and entertaining. Every number is, as always, Garnerised, but the soul of the Mighty Wurlitzer he carried incongruously within his slight frame is kept in bounds here. Jamal's trademark was eloquent minimalism, at which he was very good indeed. It depended on immaculate trio playing and pinpoint swing, and this set's exemplary. Bushkin, the least eccentric of these, was always a quite decorative, sometimes narcissistic player (if Hines was the Armstrong of the piano and Sullivan was the Wild Bill Davison, Bushkin was the Ruby Braff) but nevertheless perpetually carried a very respectable jazz kick, even when pleasing the diners.

Tatum's Shrine concert is well known. There's nothing left to say about Tatum, except perhaps that (a) the more you listen to him the less cloying he gets, because (b) he just swung more than anybody else.

DAVID PRENTICE

The landscape which stretches for many miles about this place is not the product of a spent force. If it were it would not support life. Nor is it elegant, or simple, or easy to evoke. So people tend to think only of those locations and tracks that concern their immediate purposes, while the rest dwindles, blurs out of focus. But it is possible to let the ideas of all these shapes that have evolved or been constructed on the land's surface to rear up and present themselves in their own terms, ignoring the orderings of use and convenience, and the diminutions of perspective. The concrete ramps, the angles of streets and bridges, the gardens, power cables, derelict corners, the actual hard substances the thousands of shod feet walk on every hour—these move in close and ask for acknowledgement, not of their designed shapes, which limit them, but of the unspent life which has made them and now uses them, itself in turn constrained by their forms. In a landscape seen thus, most of the people, the extras who fill the spaces in the street and the seats on the bus pass like flecks on a screen, unrecognisable. More clearly than before we see the people who are already close: the men and women we want, the men and women we have to have; ourselves. And the very complexity of personal differentiation in face, gesture, behaviour in these people can make us suddenly aware by contrast of the ground from which these variations rise. This is the substance of the human body. The body considered as a presence, without a face to make excuses or gestures to give it the appearance of meaning, with only rudimentary maleness or femaleness, the sexes parted so slightly that the attraction between them is new and constant; and violent too, because it cannot tell whether it owes its existence to difference or likeness. Useless to stand away from this presence to see it better, for it has no understanding of recession and will not play to the rules. It confronts you, implacable but not solemn, surrounding itself with whatever it wants in the way of setting—walls, water, hinged planes, chessboard pavements, ploughland even—from the crowding landscape. In closer relationship to it cluster its inevitable things; inevitable because the body must possess and must propagate. These things are very simple and small; some are unformed and germinal, while others are miniature sophisticates. Dependants of the big presence, they serve it as the supporters in heraldry serve the chief design, ministering in the capacity of seed pods, toys, children, who are their parents and their own toys. They are the little things, the early forms which help an adult one, less self contained than they, to know itself. They go along with this forceful presence, but have not the numbers or the strength to impose shape or identity on it. The only way this can be done is by making a picture.

February 1963

The Green Fuse

Where I live in the unruly turf-covered limestone hills over the Upper Dove valley the surface of the earth is eventful. The ground rucks and dives and rears itself into a rampart of peaks and sheer cliffs, tracks of the great eddies and currents of a shallow sea that was here millions of years ago. To walk or drive at ground level here is to be constantly in the company of a crowd of landmarks that rearrange themselves with every turn in the road and have to be reinterpreted with each new concealment or revelation: a world of glimpses and vistas. My nearest neighbours only a few hundred yards up the lane look out into a valley that's invisible to me; and for them the hills in the middle distance frame the same hulking moorland skyline as I see in a way that carries a different message from the one that reaches me. But peered down at from the window of an aircraft starting its descent to Manchester Airport thirty-odd miles off and still several thousand feet in the air this same landscape looks virtually flat with only a scatter of contortions in the layout of fields and an occasional wrinkle of outcrop to suggest that the flatness is illusory. The information given in this aerial view is also true but of a different order. It displays lateral relationships between sites of human activity—farms, settlements, roads, quarries—and like any comparable map such as a road atlas demonstrates fairly recent history: say a thousand or two years.

So we're down to maps, panoramas and the angles artists choose for converting the experience of the land into two dimensions. There's a common habit people have whereby it seems perfectly sane to travel by unfamiliar routes noting things of interest then on arriving home to turn immediately to the Ordnance Survey map to find where they've "really" been. The assumption that the truth must come from somewhere above the clouds dies hard, though walkers, field naturalists and those whose best insights arrive close to the ground have other views. Makers of panoramic views, in the interests of yet another truth, would impose a special set of conventions—impossibly clear air, the suppression of some of the visual effects of distance, the exaggerated sharpness of edges—in order to imply that a controlling eye could command vast amounts of detail tricked into the appearance of three dimensions: a representation of what is known to be present rather than what can be seen. These things are drawn from the highest point available, and usually with the implication of an even greater elevation, making the whole exercise appear free of gravity. In these new paintings of the hills he already knows intimately David Prentice has taken the well-documented desire to liberate himself from gravity quite literally.

(Drawing on his own experience of the flexibility of helicopter travel and the photographic record of a friend's low-level overflight of the Malverns as well as his own fascination with aerial views he has taken his eye as if some distance up into clear air to see how familiar places can be looked at afresh. The aim, and the result, are far removed from the panorama's prying eye and its tendency to provide a work of reference leading away from the picture: here the aim is to get an enhanced view of how the hills exist in a paintable space and to explore ways of pictorially rendering the vertical dimension as something different in kind rather than mere extent.

This developing exercise has now produced some effects that can seem surprising but are quite logical. In the now-familiar Malvern paintings of recent years which I think of as "heroic" or "transformational" the hill-shapes, rendered in whatever mood, are allowed to hold their own while the huge skies are the arenas for psychic-cum-visual events, skirmishes, light-fights, bars and turbulent cascades of colour. In the new paintings, however, the horizons are so high as to restrict the area of visible sky almost to nothing. A matter of angles. But the sky is in any case notionally occupied by the hovering artist and there is no room for any other dynamic. The range of colours too is less than Prentice usually offers; and there must, since he's not an artist to act on a whim, be a reason for his withholding chromatic analyses in favour of a palette almost entirely made up of arresting shades of green. The flourishing vegetation is thus everywhere faithfully and unequivocally rendered so as to play its part without distraction in the primary work of modelling the complex bulk of the ridge.

What these paintings depict is the fitting together of two elements: air, clear and often sunlit—and geology. The air is evoked in paint at various depths as the sections of the long ridge plunge, rise and swing from side to side; and the whole series explores the way the air accommodates the extraordinary shapes of the solid hills, now fully available to view. The unimaginably ancient occurrence that created the Malverns, an upthrust of molten volcanic material bursting from one of the planet's seams, is of inescapable interest, especially by virtue of its singularity. There are higher hills less impressive than the Malverns, which, seen from the old road from Birmingham by way of Droitwich and Worcester, rise over the Severn plain suddenly and emphatically and give the flat farmlands a sense of mystery-by-association that works both ways, towards and away from the hills: distances shown in many of Prentice's pictures as much more than background.

Given these potentially dramatic elementals the paintings show instead an increase in the steadiness and calm of the overview. There's almost a benign air. This sequence is quite populous, as the hills indeed are. The larger fauna of the area are out and wandering at liberty in ones and twos, wearing patches of colour. These human presences just out of facial recognition range imply no narratives: it can be assumed they are out walking for the reasons one would expect and are experiencing their own versions of what's around them. Not at all doll-like, they're occupying the space on equal terms with the artist, whose feet, it has to be assumed, have over the years also done their share in the denudation of the ridge path, seen from above as a ragged sterile scar.

Not that sterility is a theme here. Prentice found current preoccupations of his in the words of an early poem by Dylan Thomas the opening lines of which state the matter almost as pithily as it might appear in one of Blake's paradoxical epigrams: *The force that through the green fuse drives the flower / Drives my green age; that blasts the roots of the trees / Is my destroyer.*

An idea that would not have seemed strange to Blake, or to the participants in the fertility cult of the Eleusinian Mysteries with their core imageries of death and rebirth. Of interest here is the artist's having happened on such a dynamic expression of it. It is as if the mental energy that characterises virtually all his work calls for a strenuous language to contain its paradox and its crisis. He has remarked on the difficulty the suggestion of mortality has for visual art compared to writing or music. It is of course possible to make this suggestion in all three forms of art too easily and too cheaply by the manipulation of readily available stage props; but to do it with Homeric evenness probably does call for greater self-knowledge and skill in a painter. All the work in this exhibition, even the additions to the series of London paintings, can be seen as having an awareness of creation and decay: London is seen not so much as a stretch of brick and concrete assertions but as an organism continually recycling itself on its hinted-at expanse of land, with the Thames reflecting sky colours as it moves, while also sometimes taking on the colour of a stagnant canal or a slow rural river breeding life as it goes.

Anybody who practises an art learns to recognise the onset of the realisation that the work begun, in whatever medium, is failing to pull its own weight and will not be capable of generating its own continuing energy and invention. The maker can call on skill and determination to haul it along, sometimes to completion, but the knowledge that some flaw in the initial stages has generated an irremediable misdirection will rankle. Ivon Hitchens, a painter of metamorphic landscapes and also a painter of many starts, but with a keen sense of how to spot such flaws, attempted to describe his own practice at the inception of a picture.

> Setting up canvas and box in all weathers, I seek first to unravel the essential meaning of my subject, which is synonymous with its structure, and to understand my own psychological reactions to it.[1]

The primacy given here to the equation of "meaning" with structure makes it clear that the germ of purpose will point from the first in the direction of an autonomous work of art with no dangling narratives, drifts of sentiment or undigested symbolism.

The process of finding the subject by looking (objectively) and reacting (subjectively) appears to be seamless and possibly simultaneous; some elements of the process will be known to the artist and some not; and the moment of understanding may be evanescent. Great stress is thrown on the capacity and quality of the artist's imagination, the source of the "psychological reactions" the portrayal of which will wholly constitute the autonomous work of art.

These terms seem applicable to the demanding and assured way in which Prentice comes by his paintings. They can be seen to take different forms over the years as the direction of his interest varies. The pictures of hills, skies and weather that precede the newest work, for example, can evoke images of fission and collision. The force of the artist's intelligence is pitted directly against the fascinating and indestructible rock and the product of the fission is a drama of colour that enacts the collision. There's a fastidiousness at work that forbids caricature of the subject and insists that it remain honoured even when it has been given a thorough working-over in the interests of the picture. Prentice, technically accomplished to a high degree, is aware of the need to rein in a tempter he calls "the clever-dick painter", a character ready with slick effects that would satisfy any vanity the artist might have at the expense of fidelity to the subject, a quality well worth thinking about at this stage in the history of modern painting. The subject, allowing for variations and exceptions, is Nature, a term which Hitchens for example wisely takes on trust and doesn't analyse.

---

[1] Quoted in Peter Khoroche, *Ivon Hitchens,* New Ed. 2007

The tempter appears in Prentice's account of his working up of the remarkable series of water-colours in this exhibition from sketches made at the scenes. It is as if the idea of over-working immediately cancelled itself out as counter-productive, such was the pull of the subjects themselves. Described as modest, almost casual, in their inception, these pictures are much more than the products of sketching jaunts. They are a vindication of latter-day serious representational painting from the object, and coming from an artist with long experience of abstract working they have a powerful, sometimes sombre, impact and are notable exemplars of imaginative perception derived in the course of detailed observation. Mostly undertaken to capture the effect of late-winter sunlight with its habit of striking from below and simply staring, they parallel the artist's concentrated looking and also contain his confidence in having the technique to do what he wants. They are very compact. Consonances are set up that enable the images to sing, as it were, and it would be inconceivable for drag ever to set in. There's a strong sense that whatever their provenance in a comfortably parked car may have been these, as projected pictures, are portraits of moments of personal insights, even revelations, freed by masterly execution from the artist's imagination and made available to the unknown viewer. The intensity of concentration suggests the absorption of an animal, say, put into an unfamiliar space and in urgent need of reorientating itself rapidly and completely. The repeated motif of a stretch of road, often curving out of sight, emphasises Hitchens' alliance of structure and meaning and the vocabulary of leafless lichened trees, distant sunlit slopes, dark overhangs and walls makes these into landscapes of precarious fascination and desire, celebrating life, and probably framing it in a notation for mortality that satisfies the artist.

April 2010

MARY FITTON'S FORESHORES

A note for an exhibition of photographs by Mary Fitton,
'Riverbed Rotherhithe' at Oxford House, Bethnal Green, April 2013.

The camera's kindly but implacable eye gives each of these objects what looks to be a secure home, mostly on a bed of washed pebbles. They're incongruous but very much themselves and are presented not as witticisms or starters for social comment but as straightforwardly pictorial elements. For they don't much activate imaginary narratives about whatever dramas might have filled the Thames with electric toothbrushes: rather the thought-trails lead towards the design studios of maybe a decade ago or the labs of the inventors of plastics. Most of them have a quality of undisturbed purity: preserved specimens rather than cute found objects. Which is not to say they're solemn. Whereas the classic juxtapositions Duchamp and Man Ray were making a hundred years ago depended on singularity, as if a unique high-speed associational collision in a particle accelerator was shooting off energy tracks in unforeseen directions, these images, presented by the dozen, derive their effect from multiple near-repetitions. They constitute an inorganic flora like a tray of hybridising seedlings: new arrivals on a surface of immeasurably ancient little stones.

On John Cowper Powys' Letters

Early in the 1950s a friend whose interests were unfashionable and un-academic persuaded me to look out for anything I could find by John Cowper Powys. We had different points of entry and were to follow different paths through the work, a phenomenon I was to observe repeatedly as over the years I came upon others, particularly writers, who claimed to have been closely touched by it yet whose individual stakes in it were as varied as were their own writings.

I read what I could find. By 1955 there were many afternoons when once I had walked the short distance home from my work at the Blacksod (Newton Abbot in my case) Grammar School my wife Barbara and I, over tea and thin bread and butter, would take turns at reading the novels aloud to each other. In this way we read the whole of *A Glastonbury Romance* and *Porius* and large parts of *Atlantis, Autobiography* and later *The Brazen Head*. The readings were by no means solemn affairs. There was an element of vaudeville as we gave free rein to Powys' exclamatory prose with its whimsies, caperings, repetitions and indulgencies. But the work absorbed us by virtue of the combination of two qualities found nowhere else. There was the intricate portrayal of an extraordinary range of appetites, desires and obsessions: and there was the depth and sheer power of the great imaginative undertow that moves under the major novels.

I was so impressed after reading *Porius* that I took the uncharacteristic step of writing a fan letter of thanks for the experience. I knew nothing of Powys—he was not much discussed—except that he was, as it seemed then, unimaginably old and living in some sort of isolation, in Corwen as I'd heard. I rather think I wrote to him via Macdonald's. For all I knew he had little knowledge of how his work was being received. I've no recollection of my letter and hope it has not survived. I must have characterised myself as in some sense a poet as well as teacher, although my writing, no more than aimless casting about, was hardly begun. I had nothing to show and moreover knew that my own work would never resemble his. I think—I hope—I asked no questions nor gave any hint of angling for a reply, for that was far from my intention. I simply wanted tacitly to acknowledge somehow my own astonishment that there was a living mind that had so recently and unfashionably produced these ideas and that there was a publisher willing to bring them out; and also, explicitly, to let the writer know how moving I had found his profound transformation of a locality, something different in kind from the name-substitutions by which Hardy, Bennett or Faulkner gave themselves freedom to manoeuvre. A few mornings later our landlady, with a tone that suggested there was something odd, possibly disturbing, afoot, called up the stairs to say there was a letter on the hall table. I can still remember my astonishment at the sight of the envelope, addressed to the two of us in a huge and urgent hand, and the garrulous letter, sprawling and circling back on itself. It was as if the man himself had landed in our hall in a tangle of limbs and already talking. Anybody familiar with Powys' correspondence will recognise the letter as a good illustration of his technique at that time for dealing genially and immediately with mail from people he'd never heard of. I had never of course seen anything like it and it seemed a message from another world. I could be under no illusions about the quality of communication, tangential at best, carried by the content of the letter. It read like a set of answers to questions I'd not thought of asking: almost all the material was already familiar. It could have been the utterance of an oracle under compulsion to speak and to go the distance but without knowing its own focus and consequently filling space with anything to hand: in short a friendly kind of filibuster. The experience has remained unique. It was to be years before I began to meet other writers and those contacts were mundane by comparison with the sensation of having been caught sidelong by a gust of a superior energy, however light the message it carried.

There was, however, in the June letter, a small invitation to correspond, and some weeks later while staying with relatives in the Midlands I felt obliged, though with many reservations since I had nothing to contribute to the exchange, to respond to his question. I was disconcerted by the alacrity of his reply which arrived by return: a hasty note that was so obviously moved simply by the compulsion to write almost anything before the post left that I thought it best to leave that remarkable mind, with its interior connecting doors already obviously standing open, to its own better devices. I could tell he would not be writing to enquire about my silence.

June 21st 1956

[on envelope]
Mr & Mrs Roy Fisher, 90 Abbotsbury Road, Newton Abbot, Devon

[enclosed two foolscap sheets folded twice]
[page 1]

1 Waterloo
Blaenau-Ffestiniog
Merioneth
N. Wales

Thursday June 21st 1956

My dear Mr Roy Fisher
I am very proud of your excellent letter and am especially pleased at the fact that you and your wife—<u>please</u> tell me her Christian name and her surname before she became Mrs Roy Fisher—read 'Porius' with interest. You see I lived at Corwen 40 miles from here for
[2] twenty years after I came home from earning my living as a Travelling lecturer in America for over thirty years where I did my best—I quote the sarcastic words of Mr King the Upper Fourth Form master in my day at Sherborne School in Dorset—"to make Culture hum"—Almost all the real secret of Culture I learnt at Sherborne from my House Master who was Mr Martin of the Upper Fifth Form there and who wrote
[3] a History of Sherborne where King Alfred was educated and which was founded by Saint Aldhelm or AELDhelm (I can't spell it!) and who gave his name (worse spelt than my spelling!) to <u>St Alban's Head</u>—a promontory between Weymouth and Swanage well known to all the natives of Wessex. [**continues**] children and boys from 6 or 8 to 16 or 18 & I expect its *[sic]* much the same with girls often get the purpose of their whole life and the main idea of their whole life <u>at School</u>—And the importance of real education <u>there</u> is not what their teachers <u>officially</u> teach but what the children and the grown up boys <u>observe</u> (for none are more observant than the young!)
[4] really and deeply interest and thrill <u>in their own private lives</u> their teachers.

Mr W. B. Wildman was more affected by really great poetry in any tongue and by subtle points in grammar in any tongue than anyone I've ever known and it isn't anything he taught us but what we noticed obsessed him that has affected my whole life.

Now in my old age with one eye totally blind & the other only ready to work till about 9 or 10 pm and I dare not force it—if you can call your saviour and redeemer "it"!—when "it" gets exhausted because to be quite blind is my terror—so that's why I cant [sic] ramble on in letter writing as I greatly enjoy doing so my dear Mr Roy Fisher you must forgive this inadequate reply.

[Second sheet]

[5] Well! As to "Porius" the "Gaer" is a prominent ancient British camp, like "Maiden Castle" near Dorchester overhanging Corwen so I lived for 20 years under it and frequently explored it and was always dedicating my work to it & from it I could see the windings of the River Dee & the valley of Edeyrnion which between Llangollen & Llanderfel is the landscape that Ruskin said was the loveliest in Britain and which Wordsworth praised highly for all the poets used to come to write poems for and to the Ladies of Llangollen who were two

[6] grand autocratic ladies whose love for each other Wordsworth splendidly celebrated in a Sonnet he wrote to them, and who came there from Ireland.

My father the Rev C. F. Powys and my mother Mary Cowper Powys had eleven children of which your proud servant Johnny Jack was the eldest & L. C. Powys my old brother Littleton who died this last autumn, also over 80, the next, then Theodore, then Gertrude, then Nelly, then Bertie (A. R. P. the Architect) these 5 were born in Shirley Vicarage Derbyshire then to be near his mother on the death of his only brother Littleton who died in the Afgan [sic] war about 1897 [actually 1877–ed.] my father left Shirley and settled in Dorset where

[7] he luckily got a Curacy at St Peter's in Dorchester for there we used to see old William Barnes the Poet in Dorset Dialect walking about in knee breaches [sic] & silver-buckled shoes which he refused to give up. We used to go to tea at his Rectory & very soon my greatest of all poetic milestones after Mr Wildman began to be good to us—I mean the great Thomas Hardy.

At Dorchester my sister Marian the writer on how to know <u>& how to make, Lace</u> was born & also Llewelyn—then my father became Vicar of Montacute near Yeovil in Somerset where Katie (our Poetess sister) and William who now lives in Kenya and my sister Lucy were added to the Eleven of us!

[8] Gertrude became a wonderful Painter and learnt to paint at the Slade School in London & <u>then in Paris</u>. As I write I look at a picture of hers of Weymouth Bay!

I am so glad you are a poet. I began as a poet too and Macdonald's are going to publish a long poem of mine called Lucifer written in 1905 when my only child who died aged 51 a Roman Catholic Priest near Bath & is buried in the R.C. cemetery there was just about 3. I do so associate this poem <u>with that little boy</u> whom I used to walk about with in the home of my mother's relatives in Norwich and in my own home near the River Arun and Arundel in Sussex. What I got from College was purely a romantic love of the College <u>for its own sake</u>—the college to which <u>Christopher Marlowe went</u> and both my mother's father and my father's father and which is to me the most romantic college of all colleges in both Cambridge and Oxford—C.C.C.C. <u>Corpus Christi College Cambridge</u>!

[At this point the text reverts to the LH margin of Page 1, written vertically and continues on the succeeding three pages, finally returning to the upper margin of Page 1, then down its RH margin and ending in an invasion of the address.]

[#1] I think my philosophy of life today is much more heathen than it used to be. Llewelyn always was a staunch pagan and always believed that when

[#2] you were dead you were dead but <u>I was more a doubter</u> and more of a believer <u>in some sort of survival</u>, but now as I get older I come round more & more to Llewelyn's idea (which they <u>now</u> tell me, tho' he was always going to church was <u>Theodore's too</u>!)

[#3] But I would say now that what has kept me going is my <u>will</u>—I am weak and lack that <u>big jaw</u> that formidable people have but under a weak jaw I conceal an obstinate will <u>to enjoy life</u> especially now <u>as a painter would enjoy it through my one remaining eye</u>! Yes I think if there <u>were</u> such a

[##1 top] such a thing as re-incarnation—which I dogmatically à la Llewelyn's obstinate paganism refuse to believe—I should be reborn as a painter

155

[###1 RH] my favourite of all pictures is Rubens' Crucified Jesus in the National Gallery <u>from the Wallace collection</u> where Jesus looks like <u>Hercules</u> or like <u>Prometheus defying</u> both God and Man!

[####1 over address] Well I <u>must</u> stop. But my motto now is <u>Will hard enough & steadily enough and it will come whatever it is you want.</u>

Yrs   J C Powys

August 1956 [postmark]

[on envelope]
Roy Fisher Esq, 224 Broadway North, Walsall, Staffordshire

[single foolscap sheet folded twice, pages not numbered]

1 Waterloo
Blaenau-FFestiniog
Merionethshire
N. Wales

My dear Mr Fisher

I like to think of any poetical person like yourself as being connected with Birmingham for I have always associated this great Midland City with my own early memories. My father's mother my grandmother came from a family in Geneva called Moilliet a name I cant *[sic]* help associating with M. Mollet one of the French government. My grandmother Moilliet's Dad was a Banker in Birmingham and my father always spoke humorously & affectionately of this city of your birth as "Brummagem" or some word that sounded rather like that to his children's ears!

St Sulien's Well (or Julian's Well in English) is in a small cottage garden in the outskirts of Rûg (pronounced "Reeg" in English) Park the Rûg Manor House being still owned by the Wynne family cousins of the Wynnes in that park near Ruabon.

O yes I've got your Newton Abbot address if you have not changed it from 90 Abbotsbury Road (**later interpolation**—) I always associate Newton Abbot with an *[sic]* butterfly called Wood Argus but as you may have changed it I'll send this little scrawl to Walsall.

What a wonderful name Barbara Venables is! That surname Venables suggests *[on LH margin of first page]* a Church of England Bishop to me! I'm sure there was or is a Bishop of that name. Though your own surname is of course Archepiscopal!

[Sealed unsigned and concluded on verso of sealed envelope]

I did enjoy your description of that drama taught ( ) school. Do get out of your Library or get the book itself—called "What a Boy needs" by Dr Meissner of Gordonstoun School Elgin Morayshire. Published by Macdonald.

Thomas Campion

Thomas Campion (1567-1620) studied medicine and law; he was an expert musician and one of the most lucid and sure-footed of English poets. His settings of his own words have great naturalness and a freedom from clutter and the squeezing or stretching of syllables to fit. In making his songs Campion may well have exercised both crafts simultaneously. The words seem to progress by musical logic; the tunes speak. His curiosity about the possible uses of classical quantitative measures in English made him particularly alert to the effects of the crucial differences in duration between spoken and sung syllables. That interest led him into the poetry wars of the time, where he was a realistic and un-pedantic player in the exchange of polemics about the relative merits of Graeco-Roman forms and the vigorously developing native hybrids. 'Rose-cheeked Laura', from his *Observations in the Art of English Poesy*, is an illustration of his contention that a formal English lyric could hold itself together without the support either of heavy accents or bells and beeps of rhyme to emphasize the inner symmetry which should be there already. The four-line stanza, adapted from Greek, is light but instantly recognizable as a form, after which repetitions confirm and exploit it; each time with a different direction and task, so that the poem—a coherent treatise in aesthetics in sixty-odd words—quietly snakes its unpredictable way to its limpid conclusion. The falling rhythms, closer to conversation than were the powerful load-bearing iambics of the contemporary theatre, inevitably produce line-endings on unstressed syllables. Rhymed, such patterns tend to be brittle and showy: here they're confidently casual, part of the poem's light, inexorable movement, proposition by proposition, towards an exalted abstraction. Elsewhere, he's sharply sensuous and capable of rhyming with neatness and audacity.

ON A STUDY OF DADA

Alan Young: *Dada and After*
Manchester University Press (1981)

An academic work on Dada is going to look glazed and encyclopaedic or it is going to look in some degree baffled. It is to the credit of Alan Young's *Dada and After: Extremist Modernism in English Literature* that it is a work of the second kind. It doesn't lack information: the opening sections on original Dadaism and the beginnings of Surrealism are necessarily summary and made up of familiar materials, but the chapters on the English cultural scene between the two World Wars, with its tortuous reactions to those movements, presents a fresh turning-over and shaking-out of the files in a way that produces some unexpected insights.

The book is a moralized history, with the element of moralizing increasing markedly as the matters of history are progressively disposed of; it is an attempt to draw morals for present use. As history it is, to use one of the author's valued terms, "responsible" and certainly useful; as morality it is certainly suggestive, if erratic and elliptical. Young begins with a short and unexceptionable account of Dada between 1915 and 1920 in Zurich and Paris and, he stresses, in New York also. He understands how it was that Duchamp, starting from the still-new concerns of the artistic upheaval of the century's first decade, could arrive rapidly and logically at Dadaist propositions which were the natural corollaries of those very concerns; though I think he abandons that theme prematurely in favour of an emphasis on the beleaguered nihilistic wartime behaviour of the Zurich group. He succinctly characterizes the alacrity with which New York showed willingness to receive and comprehend new ideas from Europe, however disruptive and unpromising they looked; he thus prepares the ground for his later discussion of the role of America in the revival of Dada after the Second World War, and for what he then proceeds to directly: a pair of interesting, if inevitably inconsequential, chapters on the early reactions to extremist modernism in England around 1920; he deals chiefly with the Sitwells, Eliot, John Rodker, Aldous Huxley and F. S. Flint, and argues that at least the two last-named understood anti-art extremism perfectly well and rejected it, while maintaining a commitment to 'positive' modernism. That modernism might, of course, have had a better press in this country if Huxley and Flint had actively sustained their commitment for longer.

A similar service is carried out for post-Dada and Surrealism, and here the socio-literary history becomes more intricate as the time-scale lengthens. The first stage of the discussion comes in Chapter 5. 'English Critics and French Surrealism. 1922-1927', where Eliot and Wyndham Lewis are shown in more determined and articulate, though less well-informed, campaigns of rejection stimulated by the connections of Breton's Surrealism with Marxism; the explicit political claims, confused as they in fact were, serving to release and focus the energies of resistance. Young thus arrives at a turn in his account:

> The total rejection of Dadaism by the English in the twenties and, in consequence, a long delay in sympathetic interest in Surrealism, must have worked to produce a necessarily modified and weakened English version of the movement. The longer that influential English critics and writers continued in their attitude of deep hostility towards Dadaism-Surrealism (and continued to encourage a new hope in the opportunities offered either within the tradition itself or in that tradition combined with less radical modernism) the stronger such modifying and weakening effects on 'English' Surrealism would tend to be. Indeed, the question then becomes concerned not with the delay between the formation of French Surrealism and its 'arrival' in England, but with the arrival itself.

That arrival, well-chronicled in his chapters 'English Critics and post-Dada, 1927-1936' and 'Surrealism and English Literature, 1935-1950' (the latter encompassing a careful treatment of the gauche and usually unfairly vilified "New Apocalypse") is, of course, the arrival not of a fresh dynamic, a shock-wave, but of a quality diffused by the delaying action described above into something more like a tincture, a coloration, a new temperamental habiliment for that familiar figure, the British eccentric: Edward Lear, Edward Burra, the Dylan Thomas of 'The Map of Love', Stevie Smith, James Hanley, Conroy Maddox, Bruce Lacey, Cecil Collins, Ivor Cutler, Anthony Earnshaw—it would be easy to posit a British mainstream tradition made up of such figures if they were not perennially regarded as isolates, in some sense de-socialized and not of primary usefulness. The path from such an arrival to the current wide acceptability of Dadaist-Surrealist modes as constituents of a licensed, acceptable, satirical and corrective language is easy to see: it is a positive but limited use of once-revolutionary techniques. There is a further paradox arising from the delayed acceptance of those techniques in England; when Young, in the passage quoted above, refers to "opportunities offered either within the tradition itself or in that tradition combined with a less radical modernism" he is describing the habit he later accurately castigates as "our positivistic empiricism"—the practice of trimming in the middle without even looking outward to see what is at the ends. Empiricists of that sort are always liable to be intimidated by continental theorizing and to be relieved when all the issues—the aesthetics as well as the quasi-political bluster—are kept at bay by the stronger-minded locals such as Eliot and Lewis. Such vigour of repulse, acting along with, but independent of, a readiness to trivialise, makes a formidable and elusive aid to insularity.

Young's final chapter, 'Post-Dada in English Writing, 1950-1980', is the least historical and the patchiest. His method leads him to some unusually interesting questions, of the order of (my paraphrases): "By what right is Ian Hamilton Finlay as good as he so obviously is?" or "What is it about the work of Christopher Middleton that makes it seem a lost cause, and why do so few people care?" or "Why don't English poets who admire American innovations incorporate them in their own work?" (answer: "Because something in the English light turns them invisible if they do. They're all over the country, in considerable numbers—they have names like Peter Riley, J. H. Prynne, John James, Lee Harwood, Allen Fisher, Chris Torrance, Peter Philpott—and have been in copious production for up to twenty-five years; but few people know how to see them"). The questions aren't really answered, and are discussed in what seem different voices—the first generates a hagiographical tone, the second is rather muffled—but at least they are put. The urge to moralizing warps the chapter, as, indeed, it warps the book, not by its presence but by its sudden and excited appearances among otherwise wary and temperate judgments. The chapter itself begins, in ominously Buchmanite tones:

> Until the nineteen-fifties writing in Britain was able to resist successfully the worst effects of the anarcho-nihilism which to some degree had infected modernism in all the arts and which, after World War I, became a virulent disorder in Dadaism and Surrealism. Since the end of the Second World War, it can be argued, there has been a gradual, insidious spread into all levels

of British intellectual and artisric life of those more destructive and negative attitudes inherent in the modern movement.

Whatever class of thinking that represents—and Young has kept his theme in development with some subtlety—it is written as rant, and I think it false to the material. Young builds a strong case for regarding the disruptive and nihilistic features of early Dada not as fodder for latter-day kitsch but as genuinely strong meat; but his further case, for regarding the belated recrudescence of such features in an eschatological light, as a sort of terminal aesthetic, is not convincingly made: it simply occurs, as if its warrant were self-evident. It is not. In such an ambitious and wide-ranging book, this ideological rictus is a weakness. In a world that has been generated by a succession of waves emanating from the Romantic Revolution, the sort of aesthetic that proposes, once the extremists have rushed in, taken possession and perished, to move in and then deal out a little firm government on neoclassical lines is not one that everybody can find reassuring.

ON EZRA POUND

Ezra Pound was the first live poet, walking the earth and capable of having things happen to him, I ever heard of. Some of the Georgians in my school anthologies—Masefield, De la Mare—won't have been dead by 1946, but the subject of their corporeal existence didn't come up. The profession of poetry came into my view with the worst, the most succinctly dismissive press imaginable: Ezra Pound "the American poet" was a brief radio news item on the day he was declared too crazy to face trial for self-evident treason. That was the entire story as presented; sealed and done, and inviting no questions. I was fifteen; my English teacher hadn't heard of Pound, and the news coverage didn't even bother to prove his madness by quoting his poetry. I simply had the impression of a man with the nature, as well as the name, of an outlandish crank, a shabby charlatan, a small-town minor character from a Preston Sturges film gone to the bad, and not funny; Cinna the poet making a narrow escape from getting lynched.

That took care of Pound for a few years; and they were the years in which he wasn't much talked about. When, around 1950, I started to get interested in poetry, I went in through what was accessible, the untidy heap of recent insular achievers which constituted the team an English neophyte was supposed to need to come to terms with: Eliot, Auden, MacNeice, a few sideshows. Having put myself to the trouble of swallowing my aversion to much of Eliot's operation in order to elevate him into something to be revered, I was at first disconcerted to meet Pound again, shadowing Eliot and evidently working some of his more interesting strings. I read the poems, essays, harangues and letters, and formed a predictably judicious assessment. I could sense the energy and penetration of the man, but he still seemed for a while—and it's something I can't now comprehend—a lesser, more opaque figure than Eliot; and the rudimentary understanding I got of the relation between the two men lessened Eliot for me without, at first, enhancing Pound.

But as I continued reading and started writing I had to let myself understand that Pound's achievement in the second decade of the century, followed by the aspiration of *The Cantos*, made up the cliff off which everything else bounced back into play. In some way or other you had to acknowledge it. You had to touch it in order to join the game. Although there was no other route (the "English" road, which declares Pound's position irrelevant, non-existent or contrary to the national interest, has never acquired reality for me) I could see that the game didn't have to be Pound's game. When I came to know what it was he'd done I found it historically essential, and imposing, but not fascinating. It gave me orientation, especially insofar as it exemplified the notion of doing something as well as it can possibly be done (notwithstanding all the archaic assumptions about self-appointed vicarious heroism that implies) but it didn't draw me in.

For one thing, there was the question of timing. By the mid-century Pound was an abstraction, at first physically removed, then silent, the work left to die. Allying oneself to an abstraction has a smell of religious danger; something that evidently wasn't present twenty years earlier, in the enviable times when Zukofsky, Oppen, Bunting and Rakosi could be part of the current action.

I was also pretty clear that Pound's aesthetic, mixing perennialism with rubble, was something I could see, but not follow. I could bring nothing to it; nor could it directly serve my own work, which I was in the event to reach by way of Williams, not Pound. In language my specialism is in the pathology of soft tissues, transient and perishable substances; when it comes to bone I'm out of my element. I'll still turn to Pound for a reminder of what hardness is.

DEBT TO MR BUNTING

My first sight of Basil Bunting's poetry was in manuscript: the handwriting was Gael Turnbull's. At our first meeting, in the autumn of 1956, Gael showed me a manuscript book in which it was his habit to copy, partly for preservation, partly for closer acquaintance, poems that from time to time caught his interest. The selection was varied, but uniformly unfashionable, and almost wholly unavailable to English readers at the time. The book contained 'The Orotava Road' and 'The Well of Lycopolis', transcribed from a borrowed copy of the Galveston collection. The author's name was unfamiliar, though I should have recognized it from Pound's published correspondence; and I'd not then seen Pound's anthology. Gael, who had yet to call on him in Throckley, could tell me little beyond the frustrating story of the Gleaner's Press publication, itself a badge of inaccessibility that deepened what looked like the fated obscurity of the poet's career. The two poems, however, came through with great clarity, and with a tone I was glad to recognize, having been unconsciously listening out for it for some years. The tone was one of plain authority: of a man with his ideas and his idiom sorted out and within easy reach, so that a quite matter-of-fact way of proceeding held great force and definition. I suppose what I'd been after was writing that showed not the oddity of poetry-as-against-common-language that takes the form of incrustations of manner, but the true oddity, the critically fine distance between the two within which an energy-field is created and maintained.

The Bunting poems were from the Thirties but not *of* the Thirties in the sense in which that period was commonly understood. And they lacked the tendency to prance which poetry from England had displayed then and was still showing in the Fifties. The post-*Mauberley* gestures of 'The Well of Lycopolis' were, of course, apparent; but I was more taken with the poem's eloquent scruffiness, done with appetite and familiarity. Also my contact with the poetry was eased and made more immediate, I later understood, by certain important absences. Metaphysics. "Self expression". Bogus entities. Declamatory or baroque diction—there are plenty of resonant, even strident, phrases in Bunting, but they have a way of appearing to come up from under, generated by compression, rather than being caught from the air above and decanted. Those absences, on the nature of which Basil was happy to expand once people had begun asking his opinions, were liberating. I was in no position yet, though, to learn practical lessons from what I saw that day. I had published one rather monstrous short poem, and the work I was engaged on was preposterous. All I had was fluency and an ambition for grand effects of fantasy. Nevertheless, in the years that followed, during which I started to find material I could handle and worked out some techniques for doing so with less fuss, I grew better acquainted with Basil's work and heard Gael Turnbull and Michael Shayer's reports on their contacts with him. He was said to be busying himself with the recovery and destruction of as many of his letters as he could get his correspondents to part with: a sign he was taking himself seriously. I got to take a turn with one of the small number of unbound copies of the Cleaner's Press book that were somehow in circulation, and I read 'The Spoils' before it was published.

I met Basil Bunting for the first time in the late spring of 1965 in Michael and Ebba Shayer's flat in Worcester. Half a dozen or so people were invited—I can remember the poets John James, Michael Butler and Nick Wayte—to hear Basil read 'Briggflatts'. At that time he was a greyer and less imposing presence then he later became, in the years when he came to look like a possibly, but by no means certainly, retired adventurer. Then, and for some years to come, he was not in effective eye contact with people, distanced by the increasing blindness caused by cataracts. He was quiet, affable and assured, and his reading, in the Shayers' living room was firm without being projected. The poem was clearly something formidable, and we were all still at its edge.

One of us asked him whether it was complete, and I can remember saying to somebody afterwards that I found his reply and its manner shocking. This is not to say I was repelled: merely intellectually disturbed. With no hint of whimsy or a wish to provoke, he'd said the music was complete but the content still required adjustments here and there. I was to come to an understanding of what he meant, and of the reasons he had for his arrangement of priorities; but at the time I was not braced for such a blow about the head. I'd brought my own work by then into something of a focus, but couldn't hold it there. I'd fallen temporarily out of love with the English language, hearing only its deliquescence into an infinitely supple slither, well on the way to becoming nothing more than worldwide Airport English. With my back to the wall I was planning a diction that would allow such concepts as it could carry to be translated frictionlessly from one language to another, and then another, without regard for sound. This would have represented a total flight from Basil's Dantean view of language, on which I would later place a decent reliance. About his ready use of the idea of musicality I was more sceptical, and remain so to a degree, even though I've heard, and read, his and others' explanations of it. As a musician I use the term myself, but that's only to say that *I* know what I mean by it. I wouldn't put it forward as analysable.

Hearing Basil converse, and particularly hearing him read from texts constructed to display sound patterns, I was immediately jealous of the luck that had taken one of the Buntings so far north. Had Basil been born, like his father, on the East Midland coalfield he would have been harder put to it to find a language to write in. I was jealous most of all of the northern survival of tough consonants, by now optional at best in the Midlands and South, but still in place for him, and able to trigger resonant and resilient vowels. For a Midlander, long out of earshot of any ancestral voices that might once have sounded in Repton crypt, there was nothing to be done about this loss beyond dealing the syllables as cleanly as possible and keeping the Latinisms in bounds.

I never had the temerity to show Basil a poem of mine for comment, for I knew that to creep unseen past my own inhibitions about writing at all I always had to travel light in the matter of craft and permanency. What I did would have been unlikely to engage his interest, and I've no idea whether he ever looked at it. Nevertheless, he was often there when I gave readings, and I found his presence benign and heartening rather than intimidating. There was one occasion when he made a compliment. I'd read my 'Three Ceremonial Poems', and these he singled out as being free of what he called "philosophising". I still hear that remark, even though I may discount it, whenever I lose patience and decide to let myself prate. His views hardly needed articulating. I sat once at a table in Stuart and Deirdre Montgomery's flat overlooking Southampton Row, correcting the galleys of 'City' for the Fulcrum Press *Collected Poems 1968,* with Basil sitting quietly in the corner peering at *The Times* with the pages held close to his face. Every time I looked in his direction I felt for an adjective to cut or a construction to contract. It was the nearest I could get to asking for a blessing on my prose.

Sometime in the mid-Seventies I turned up to give a reading at a fairly new and fashionable university. My student host was a bright, optimistic young woman, running a well-organized reading series. I asked who the other poets were and she named the names of the day. Then:

—We *did* invite Basil Bunting.

—And he sent you a dreadful letter that made you cry.

—Well yes!

—I hope you sold it for a lot of money?

—*I tore it up and flushed it down the loo!*

To abash girls and bring them out in pentameters was probably not Basil's aim. Nevertheless, his standard refusal-note, in some such terms as that poets should not have to peddle their wares for mean fees in the public markets, must have had that effect more than once, for he seemed to deliver it with renewed vehemence each time. When he chose, he could be generous. At about the same time, Eric Mottram and I tutored a course at Lumb Bank and invited Basil to be guest reader, a two-hour engagement, modestly paid. He arrived early, and left only on the third day, having given two long evening readings, one from his own work and another, gratis, from Wordsworth, Wyatt, Tennyson, and Swinburne, and conversed amiably and usefully with anybody who wanted to talk to him.

He had a variable attitude to his paymasters and benefactors, quite often prickly, particularly when the assistance came from official quarters or from those who would sentimentalize him, for he was a very tough man. He kept ready to hand a shifting *persona,* made up from a cast of archaic roles—the medieval mendicant poet, the cultured Imperial slave, the dispossessed exile—and employed it from time to time in whatever way suited him. I think it gave him some continuity: a device for steering his way through a life that was made up of an unending series of predicaments, some exciting and colourful, some quite desolate and, on the surface at least, pitiable.

The atavistic *persona* was less profound than the archaisms that show in the poetry. These encompass, but go far beyond, the general craving of Modernism to be understood by the past: they express an extraordinarily sustained faith in the stability and perennial utility of properly-made works of art. His pantheon was small, and will be familiar to all his readers, but it was composed only of works and practitioners that had been subjected by him to rigorous and repeated testing. It was assembled not to impress or browbeat, but for his own use lifelong. The institutionalized revisionism that provides the oxygen-supply of academies will not have engaged him at all.

I believe the more desolate of his predicaments give an insight into what drove his work. When I got to know him reasonably well I always got the impression that he'd been born a vigorous, contradictory hybrid and made himself as comfortable as he could with his natures, progressively organizing himself into the craggily gracious old ruffian of the last decade or so. I never sought to get on to the level of personal confidences with him, but I set great store by knowing him and always enjoyed any contact. He was the only literary figure I've ever met who produced in me the sort of incredulous awe I'd get from, say, shaking hands with Earl Hines—and it wasn't just a matter of the words on the page. Along with the affable, anecdotal man one met there was something that remains to me inscrutable. On the one hand there was the high and genuine sense of artistic standard, respect and ethics. But there was also the inaccessible sense of a demon of delinquency and improvidence—the absences, the goings-to-ground, the impulsive initiatives, the periods of yielding to circumstance in a curiously—I'm tempted to say suspiciously—passive manner. A sort of anti-matter countering the will to achieve good things, and in some way ministering to it. Not that he was secretive. He would fish many a story out of those strange periods but I, at least, never heard him engage in any retrospective self-analysis or evaluation about how they happened.

When Basil died I was finishing work on a long poem, 'A Furnace', which I'd felt obliged to write, come what may. Nobody sane would court comparison with a work so defiantly strong-tasting as Basil's, and my poem was by its nature more nebulous, and I worked on it with no thought of homage to 'Briggflatts'. But I can make two observations. The first is that I noticed, rather ruefully, that it had taken me twice the length of 'Briggflatts' to locate the relationships in my material and make something like a poem out of it. The second is that had 'Briggflatts' not succeeded formally I'd have been unable to conceive of my poem at all. Impossible Poetics are all around, spreading old-style transcendental menace along with distant hope. The value of Basil's poetic was that it was difficult but possible. There are probably many of us who refer to that idea, as he embodied it, even though our work doesn't overlap at all with his, or with one another's.

At a Tangent

It will have been some time in the years after the institution dissolved itself that I failed the entrance test for Black Mountain College. I was to learn years afterwards that my first hearing of the place's existence, in the summer of 1956, coincided, possibly to the day, with the site's final manifestation of any note, the production of Robert Duncan's *Medea*. At that time I also had sight of the numbers of *Black Mountain Review* that had so far appeared, and they gave an almost coherent impression of a compact powerhouse of activity: news of the real situation was scarce and hard to interpret. It was only as time passed that Olson's conception of the college's work as centrifugal rather than centripetal came to be visible in the works and careers of the *diaspora*. The Black Mountain College of the first half of the 1950s had been more an up-country salon of ad hoc gatherings at its summer Institutes, gatherings that had strengthened the work of the remarkable individuals who came and went.

The impact of the ideas current and made identifiable in that period was powerful and liberating and many of them still seem to me essential. There will have been a number of us, unknown to one another and widely dispersed, who found they had been living inside an imagined egg that was suddenly shattered; and the news was quickly taken in and shared around, chiefly by letter. I soon fell into correspondence with Cid Corman in Matera, Larry Eigner in Swampscott and Denise Levertov somewhere on the move. I'd hardly begun writing and had met no writers other than Gael Turnbull, who had started the whole American thing off for me, and it would be a few years before I met Jonathan Williams and Creeley. (Duncan and Cage came later still. I never met Olson, encountered Dorn too late, and never had direct contact with Fielding Dawson even when I met him).

The effect of all this on what I was doing was curious. Starting in my teens from an interest in surrealism I was always on the lookout for anything odd, neglected or forbidden. By the mid-Fifties I was devoted to quietly deranging my imagination in the direction of escapist fantasies and my relation to reality wasn't in good shape, apart from holding down a job. The grandiose and unpublishable poems I wrote were just by-products. The Black Mountain insight let in some air and daylight. It was a relief from myself to be able to try a run of casual poems that originated nowhere in particular, and some of them came out clean enough to keep. One effect

I remember is the way that paper seemed to have changed its nature for me. It was alive, suggestive and various and asked to be written on in all sorts of ways.

I was in part liberated by Black Mountain, but in other ways ill-equipped to run with its causes. What I already knew of Pound and Williams was snapped into focus; there was a partial revelation of the Objectivists, congenial to me but not yet reawakened. But I wasn't able to work consistently and my mind threw up distractions. And I suppose I was more wary than I need have been of something I thought I detected among the mannered urgencies of the Olson-Creeley communications: an old-style Romantic Absolute, even a purism I'd have to avoid at all costs. I could do mimicry (and I was to witness in the Sixties some marvellously misdirected English imitations of the surfaces of both Creeley and Olson) but I knew that, as a born caricaturist and *bricoleur*, any attempt of mine to affect purism would simply be cheesy.

At a tangent: decades later, playing the piano to accompany singers who liked to do the Bessie Smith Songbook I'd hear these words: *back in Black Mountain a child will slap your face; the babies cry for liquor, and all the birds sing bass.*

ON A STUDY OF ROBERT CREELEY

Cynthia Dubin Edelberg,
Robert Creeley's Poetry: A Critical Introduction
University of New Mexico Press (1978)

As a survey of the first twenty-five years or so of Creeley's work, and as an exercise in the placing of themes and techniques, this book is useful and timely; as an attempt to make sense of him by a mixture of biography and analysis, it overreaches itself and sometimes displays a bright, respectful critical automatism which simply fails to match up to the toughness and perpetual elusiveness of the subject.

The problems of characterizing Creeley's achievement at fifty are considerable. We might get some perspective on them by setting him alongside Robert Frost at a similar stage in life, and looking for the common factors: an absence of precocity; disqualifications from easy entry into the academic or literary swim; the establishment of an immediately recognizable personal style characterized by meticulous control; the appearance of having, over and over again, conjured subject-matter from unexpected sources; the exploration of moral disquiet and of unspecified personal distress; an academic acceptability which developed late but gave, or imposed, a life-style at odds with the poetic *persona*. Carrying this comparison any further would only magnify its grotesqueness; I make it in order to suggest that it is now becoming possible to sentimentalize Creeley for similar reasons to those which made the sentimentalization of Frost almost inevitable, though, without, of course, the powerful assistance to the process which Frost himself gave.

Dr. Edelberg's text is dense, expert and pretty technical, and exists in healthily close relationship with her main sources—the poems, the writings collected in *A Quick Graph,* Donald Allen's *Contexts of Poetry* and Mary Novik's *Robert Creeley: An Inventory, 1945-1970*—but implicit in her commentary, and showing through here and there, there seems to me to be a will-to-order which may be stated in some such terms as the following: the poet suffered misfortunes in early childhood which caused him emotional damage and gave him particular difficulty in his attitudes to, and relationships with, women. His attempts, often confused, to solve such problems, especially those arising from his first marriage, generated the special qualities of the poems, collected in *The Charm* and *For Love,* which made his reputation. Socialized and made more confident by success and remarriage, he shifted attention in *Words* to the creative process, achieving greater technical fluency; then, in *Pieces,* he "understood" that he had developed to a point where he was free from what had seemed to him some of the imperatives of the earlier work, and could safely use more extended, less tense forms, a progress continued in *A Day Book*. Equipped with this self-knowledge, he now exhibits, by his example, the rewards of patience and of the acquisition of a more existential outlook.

Such an approach tells the wrong story: it is really unnecessary to look for so much synthesis, or for much in the way of biographical determinants, in a body of work so strenuously elliptical and under so much internal, aesthetic, pressure to shift its ground. Dr. Edelberg's study allows for an assessment of these forces but does not engage with them directly enough.

ON KENNETH REXROTH

Kenneth Rexroth, *An Autobiographical Novel*
Whittet Press (1977)

Substantial sections of Kenneth Rexroth's *An Autobiographical Novel* appeared in this country in 1972 as the first quarter of Eric Mottram's valuable *The Rexroth Reader;* we now have a British edition of the full text as published by New Directions in 1966, seven years or so after the main period of its composition.

That period is of some importance. In the late 1950s Rexroth had been in San Francisco for thirty years and had been continuously active in the artistic life of the area; he was now living through a time of great vitality in the work of those surrounding him, and had a significant role as a guide, promoter, point of reference, and provider of information. He was working with Lawrence Ferlinghetti and various musicians on a series of highly successful poetry-with-jazz presentations and the *Autobiographical Novel* was, in origin at least, an oral composition, spoken into a tape-recorder and edited by re-recording before the tapes were handed over to amanuenses. There is a principle at work—"I admire Defoe and the great Chinese novelists and I have spent my life striving to write the way I talk"—but it is not oppressive, since Rexroth's manner is flexible and direct; and the mode of the book is for the most part a fairly expansive narrative laced with opinions. It is in fact a mode not far removed from that of the long autobiographical poems, 'The Dragon and the Unicorn' and 'The Heart's Garden, the Garden's Heart' on the one hand, or, on the other, from that of many of Rexroth's most characteristic essays: the writer's role of mediation between the world of his experience and the reader is pretty much the same in all the genres. This is where the usefulness of the *Autobiographical Novel* to the understanding of Rexroth's achievement lies. By its bulk and concentration it anchors a body of work which can otherwise seem drier and less substantial than it ought, given the keenness of Rexroth's perception, the consistency of his dedication and the prodigality of his experience. The balance of Mottram's selection in *The Rexroth Reader* showed this function of the prose reminiscences very well.

There is not much to be said about the use of "novel" in the title; it is not an important part of the reader's experience of the book and its presence is rather puzzling. Some characters—notably Rexroth's first wife—are given invented names, presumably for the usual reasons for such masking, but with no clear rationale. An odd example is the account of the drummer Dave Tough who appears, perfectly recognizable, but with his name caricatured in the manner of Kerouac, as "Dick Rough"; while earlier in the book he is mentioned under his real name. This is careless editing, but it is also clear that Rexroth never takes useful advantage of the releases from entailment offered by a fictional approach. His characteristic tone is that of a rational and considered account of varied and often extraordinary experiences; it is a tone which can recall that of H.G. Wells—one of Rexroth's strongest and most interesting influences—in *An Experiment in Autobiography*, even though he claims not to have used his own personality as material in the way Wells did: "I have always been too busy being a poet or a painter or a husband or a father or a cook or a mountain climber to worry about my personality, and this book is my first attempt to consider it at all. Reading the typescript over I discover that it is largely straight factual narrative, a great deal of it about other people."

That passage locates the paradox which makes the book unusually valuable. It is a chronicle rather than a self-analysis, but it is a chronicle of American events which seem in the telling to have thrust themselves on the attention of a boy who is often idealistic but whose life appears never to have allowed him a single moment of innocence. Throughout the sequence of anecdotes, portraits and reflections runs a pair of common assumptions: that the subject needs at all times to be able to size up his situation quickly, and that he always has the means of doing so at his disposal. If the story has a form it is picaresque, in that the hero is initiated in various ways, is jailed, beaten, has periods of success as a charlatan as well as a genuine entertainer and artist, undergoes sexual experiences ranging from the romantic to the sudden and grotesque, and so forth; but it is also a chronicle of decisions, about value and about what to do next, and the adventurer is after something more than the exercise of his curiosity and his appetite for life. The changes of direction seem capricious as they are presented, and his assessments of them can look contradictory: by turns he experiences great happiness as a celebrant of Chicago life, as a lover, as a Forest Service patrolman on the Pacific coast, as a celibate near-novice in an Anglo-Catholic monastery, as a horse-wrangler, as a husband; but the roles as they are successively taken up are obviously elements in an eccentric programme of personal development rather than a linear, selective career. Over and over again his precocious faculty for judgment leads him to back away from forms of acceptance and success which he feels inappropriate, whether the temptations come from the school honours system, Marxism, sexual flattery, domesticity, organized crime, or the literary hierarchies.

It needs to be remembered that Rexroth is working over his material at a generation's remove. His book is the work of a man born in 1905 describing his first twenty-one years with the declared aim, as he says, "of leaving a record for my young daughters of what my own youth had been like." Merely as an eyewitness report of the life and times of a shrewd, imaginative and hyperactive adolescent in the Chicago area and New York City in the early twenties it is of great interest, and there is no space here to begin to sift the legions of names he drops, sometimes with discrimination, sometimes in the manner of a burlesque, as in his account of the Loebs' salon on page 130. He drops his story at the moment of his settling in San Francisco in about 1926, and barely refers to any subsequent events. But the book's strong ethical strain takes no account of this gap; the autobiographer and his young subject live by the same standards, but in the light of an idea which Rexroth put most strongly in an essay on Kenneth Patchen: "Imagine if suddenly the men of 1900— H. G. Wells, Bernard Shaw, Peter Kropotkin, Romain Rolland, Martin Nexo, Maxim Gorky, Jack London—had been caught up, unprepared and uncompromised, fifty years into the terrible future. Patchen speaks as they would have spoken, in terms of unqualified horror and rejection." The names in that list are part of the young Rexroth's programme of self-education, and that programme, documented in detail throughout *An Autobiographical Novel,* is probably fairly typical of what was likely to engage a committed autodidact of that time and place. Very few of the names in the programme are American, though the stamp of the whole enterprise and its result is thoroughly so. Rexroth can easily be fitted into the now commonly taught pattern of an American tradition, but he signally ignores that idea, with its connotations of an increasingly self-regarding progression of cultural moments. If he lives out episodes from Thoreau or from Twain—as in his long verbatim reproduction of his health-food booklet *spiel*—he does so without acknowledgment or allegiance, except to the implicit guidelines acquired from his own family. "Most American families that go back to the early nineteenth century, and certainly those whose traditions go back to the settlement of the country, have a sense of social and cultural rather than nationalistic responsibility. The sense that the country is really theirs, really belongs to them, produces radical critics, rebels, reformers, eccentrics."

GAEL TURNBULL

I heard that Charles Tomlinson's first response to the news of Gael Turnbull's sudden death was, "I owe everything to Gael!" Those words could have been mine. Gael was my friend for almost fifty years and without his interest I would have foundered early. To instruct, or even guide, was not his way. Instead he would simply bear you company through unmapped territory across which he too had his path to find. After some years you would find yourself in an unsuspected clearing where you could proceed to work in your own way. This is what happened to me. Gael still stayed near, entertained by the divergence in our writings. He marked it by maintaining, by means of a stream of cuttings, the fiction that without ever leaving town I was the secret author of the *Nature Jottings* in every newspaper he came across.

Of all my lost friends he is the least dead. The unique pace of his mind, sometimes troubled, always curious, seems still to be keeping us company somewhere just out of reach.

2006

Foreword to *Spleen*
(Baudelaire / Nicholas Moore)

"One thing led to another" said Nicholas Moore by way of explanation of his multiple version of Baudelaire's poem which, although not a sonnet, behaves like one, turning out to be capable of having its form reused, over and over again, without being exhausted. For Moore on this occasion the form to be repeated wasn't just the eighteen-line matrix: it was also Baudelaire's armature of notions, the fixed sequence of a dozen or so tropes which expand the master-simile of the opening line. Over and over again Moore inserts himself into the narrow space between the terms of the simile, the "I" and the "king", and, once in, is free to rove without inhibition through the waiting figures, which he tackles each time as a series of picaresque challenges, ducking his way through, scoring wherever he can and sometimes not being too proud to wriggle his way out by way of the final couplet without making too much of a work of art of it all.

The knowledge that each version is one of many lets him off the hook of a service-translator's convergent caution and frees him from what would otherwise have been a deadening task, the attempt to reproduce in any one version what I take to be the steady, contained tone of the original. That disposition shows up here and there in Moore's versions, and something like it is apparent overall; but the baroque assemblage which is the complete work shows how containment, a drawing-in of a set of conjured images to fix a self-image, wasn't to Moore's purpose. In his sequence, it is by the compulsion to repeat the same gestures that the self—which is not Baudelaire's "I" any more than the beasts, the clown, the bed are Baudelaire's—is fixed. Baudelaire's king can't play; all Moore's kings can, for a brief space this side of the absinthe-green waters of Lethe. And they must: it's like a mass audition of theatre directors, each allotted five minutes to market his "interpretation" of the same classic.

Moore has his tropes point outwards to form a chaotic, knockabout world very different from Baudelaire's metered, Poe-like management of types. They're often loose, and perky, and they take wild satirical swipes; the tone is seldom even. I imagine most English speakers will have their reading of the French accompanied by an unworded, spectral version of the English "meaning"; when I read Moore, I can feel his capering language working over that grey sub-English in my head, and I'm reminded of Hugh MacDiarmid's or Robert Garioch's way of twisting English so as to compel it, against its inclination, to make Scottish points.

This curious work gives something of a paradigm of the way Moore worked from his personal isolation. Striking repeatedly at a set of concepts—which happen not quite to be obsessions of his own—he produces deliberate variations, in the course of which, and around which, he populates the space about him—a space which sometimes seems dark, at others pallid as the paper of a cartoon—with fantastic personages, of no particular shapes or sizes and no consistent relation to reality. Although Moore's stake in the game, the "I" he substitutes for Baudelaire's, is characterised clearly enough as the sequence proceeds, it's relieved of autobiographical dead weight by his evident lack of possessiveness about his own name and identity. He allows himself to be liable, chiefly by anagram (Conilho Moraes, Alonso Moriches, Rosine MacCoolh, Lhoso Cinaremo) to the same casual mutations as befall Alan Bold, Chatto and Windus, Richard Rodney Bennett, Mickey Spillane, Lord Goodman, Al Alvarez, Giacometti, Auden and the rest. The cast is heterogeneous and the criteria for it remain inscrutable: a naturalist, James Fisher, and a psychiatrist, Henry Yellowlees, turn up, as well as J. W. Lambert and Maurice Wiggin, *Sunday Times* writers of the period, and, quite possibly, the Motown singer Cindy Birdsong. There's no specific tone or direction to the "black fun": it inhabits the classic bleak world of the satirist, where rudderless impulses for good struggle among scoundrels and impostors, and there's also an element of the wacky, knuckle-cracking, self-generated glee of the isolate who's not sure whether there's really anybody out there waiting to share his jokes.

For me, Nicholas Moore disappeared from view in the early 1950s, and the only indication I had of his continuing existence was, over the last ten or fifteen years of his life, the frequent mention of his name on the BBC Radio Three weekly *Jazz Record Request* programme; he was probably its most persistent client. So far as I remember, the records he asked for would be fairly venerable but never hackneyed. For anyone who knows the music, his borrowing for a pseudonym in 1945 of the name of the quite obscure black trumpeter Guy Kelly will give a good idea of his taste: Kelly's music was nervous, intense and plaintive; he played on a handful of memorable records in 1936 and died young. The jazz references in *Spleen* are affectionate and honorific; each is a talisman against the universal slither. Bessie Smith's *Cold in Hand Blues* crops up in the text on equal terms with phrases from Marvell and Shirley. Among the titles and marginalia, *Tail Sting Blues* is adapted from the Mound City Blue Blowers' *Tail Spin Blues*; "Edward Kennedy Hellowell" shares forenames with Duke Ellington; Lester Young and Willie the Lion Smith are only lightly disguised, while Peewee Russell, Yusuf Lateef and Dick Wilson (again hardly a household name: he was tenor saxophonist in Andy Kirk's Twelve Clouds of Joy in the 1930s) appear as themselves.

Moore's *Spleen* is a barrage of signs of life and mischief. Helpless enough in the circumstances of his life, he was in no sense helpless before his gift, nor was he diffident or unknowing about his craft or purpose. In the posthumous collection *Lacrimae Rerum* there is superb poetry which can move in an instant from clear prose sense to unforced lyric, and back again; both of them tones unfamiliar in modern English. These versions show another part of the same enterprise.

February 1990

INTRODUCTION TO *SELECTED POEMS* BY JEFF NUTTALL

"Breakfast at Guernsey Grove" catches, on more levels than one, a moment of Eric Mottram's hospitality. Anybody who stayed, as I often did in the Sixties, at Eric's previous place, the basement flat on Kensington Church Street, will have had the experience of being allowed, around 3 a.m., to give up and doss down on the couch in the living room. The last thing I'd see as I reached for the light-switch across the great bedside pile of books my host had assembled against the impossible event of my getting insomnia, was an object by Jeff Nuttall that watched from the top corner of a tall bookcase. It was an overfilled-to-bursting doctor's bag, a dusty Gladstone from which viscera, rubber things and respirator hoses bulged, apparently caught, though possibly only temporarily, in the act of escaping. Satirical? Not really. Observant. Extravagant. Wary. It was my first meeting with Jeff Nuttall's work and it was an accurate guide to most of the multifarious ranging of his activities. Besides "art" there was of course theatre—the Quack Doctor from hundreds of years of mummers' plays and the hint of a future Friar Tuck to rival Eugene Palette's.

And there was already the abiding theme, to be found everywhere in this collection, of the politics of boundary and containment, and the aesthetics of that zone, something like the sea-bed fissures out of which magma continuously steams and smokes to create the world. In human terms there's always the assumption of the precariousness and the permeability of the self's temporary packaging: the brain-box, the bone-locker, the bag of guts, all miraculous, all vulnerable, all capable of breaking bounds and messing up the moquette.

Like any life-forms that aren't pickled in jars these poems draw on their manifest energy for their form. Particularly interesting are the poems that have empirical reference: locations, for example, that another consciousness could check against experience or assumption. And in doing so probably apprehend with unusual emphasis what a variety of different worlds our familiar individual aesthetics look out.

2003

Concerning Joseph Brodsky

1.

My initial reaction to Joseph Brodsky's London and Florence poems was an extra-textual one: that one shouldn't pander to the pretensions of historic capitals and city-states by honouring them with poetic set pieces, however brilliant. If the poet who does that is merely a cultural tourist the work will have a stale smell. But it's plain in all of these poems that Brodsky is a genuine stranger who has a right—indeed he has no choice but to do so—to bring himself from the city of his birth to these particular "sacred" places and measure them as parts of a deeper journey. So he's a constant presence. You're aware of him looking from under lowered lids at what these showplaces are showing him; and you're also aware that at the same time he's drawing his own pictures of them by mapping them in similes and metaphors, sometimes outrageous. Characteristically, he goes for the monumental self-images of the places, especially Washington, but isn't overawed. Also, he sets out in Florence to conjure Dante, and has enough strength of will to bring it off. Not many would have managed it.

It's in the second of the remarkable pair of stanzas—the fourth and fifth—of 'The Thames at Chelsea', where he shrugs free of the patterned tedium of London and dives into his own compulsions, that I find most common ground with Brodsky's writing about cities. I don't imagine he'll ever now need to write about a city like mine, a huge, hasty, uncherished growth with no metropolitan qualities and only the shallowest claims on imperial history, but having for all that the power to overwhelm a poet's consciousness. I'd like to see what he'd do with it.

2.

I can't comment on the sound of Brodsky's Russian as it compares with other Russian poetry which may be considered less prosaic. And, paradoxically, his perpetual play of metaphor and other figures shows up in the English version as a texture much more ornately worked and eventful than the low-mimetic or conversational quality of most contemporary poetry written in English. So we have to take the alleged prosaic element on trust. Where it is unmistakably present for us is in the persona: the pace of its attention, its dryness, its irony. Devices are used, not to inflate but to maintain a constant process of deft conceptual housekeeping. The lyric sense is always there, but its flights are kept short.

3.

An important part of language has to do with the familiar notion that an authoritarian state can steal the people's language and then, since language is extremely vulnerable to taboo, lease it back in a doctored condition, using it as an instrument of social and mental control. Any scraps of deviant language cannot then but acquire magical powers—real powers, too, to strike fear into the authorities, to change events, to get people killed— whereas with us language comes cheap and is thought to be plentiful and hence unremarkable. Brodsky doesn't appear in his poems as a romantic or dramatized figure, but his poetic impetus comes from an underlying dramatization of his magical and intimate relationship with the powers, and the fate, of the Russian language.

4.

After writing my poem 'The Collection of Things' earlier this year I became aware that while describing a scene into which I could easily imagine Brodsky walking I had been sailing not far from some of his concerns. Apart from Life, Death and Time, I can detect such themes as the survival of poets as monuments; the preservation and revival of classical ceremonies (the Delphic Festivals which Sikelianos instituted); the mission of poetry and language to lead the consciousness of nations; cultural pilgrimage. There's even a mention, rare for me, of Judaeo-Christian beliefs. Some things—love, metre and rhyme—I couldn't manage to include on this occasion.

5.

First, let me say that I'm unqualified to attempt questions about Brodsky's reputation in the English-speaking world since I don't like to read reputationist journals. But my impression is that the answer has to be "no". Brodsky is inevitably, and correctly, seen as allying himself with his great predecessors across the half-century which separated his birth from theirs—a gap unoccupied, so far as my knowledge goes, by any poets of sufficient stature to connect the generations. I think the importance of the earlier group was appreciated by English-speaking writers only after about 1960, and largely posthumously; even Pasternak was dead almost as soon as translations and anecdotes in the wake of the *Zhivago* affair made him world-famous. It took extra-poetic events of that sort, including the belated appearance of biographical information about those writers' personal fates, to turn them into dramatic characters who could be idealized and, from a safe distance, envied for the dedicated hostility and the dedicated adulation their culture accorded them. No poet in the West could find or engineer such concentration; nor do we have any poets of that generation capable of being considered, in retrospect, heroic in that way. In the relatively trivial terms of reputation, leaving merit out of it, Brodsky was rather at a disadvantage by virtue of being (a) a postscript, (b) alive, (c) vociferous and, (d) after his early misfortunes, apparently well looked-after—latterly, merely to belong to the Super-League (Brodsky, Walcott, Murray, Heaney, Milosz) tended to attract an automatic assumption of over-valuation.

6.

I know no Russian. Brodsky's self-translations are offered, like anyone else's, as English poems "after the Russian of Joseph Brodsky", and as English poems I'm generally uncomfortable with them. My discomfort's a common one. While it's clear that he's gone to great and ingenious lengths to attempt the impossible—to indicate the complexity of the relation of his highly figurative invention to the natural (Russian) language which generated it and with which it constantly plays—the work is often spoilt for me by his insistence on forcing his metaphysical beliefs about metre, and particularly rhyme, on a language which won't accept them without audible protest, thus producing a degree of grotesqueness which must, I feel, go beyond the level of idiosyncracy which, as his characteristic patterns of thought suggest, really did need to be brought across from the Russian—something in which he was apparently successful. And it's worth saying that Brodsky was a fluent, sure-footed and engaging writer of English prose.

But every discrete human language has its own ways of generating its specialized formal modes. English has, as well as a rigorously regulated dependence of meaning on word order, subtleties of quantity, intonation and the varied qualities of regional and class sub-dialects which raise constant challenges for writers—particularly poets—engaged in notating them finely. Of the parallelisms used in English poetry, end-rhyme is the coarsest and probably, after some seven hundred years, the most debased: it's not now a subject for a mystique. The implications of any instance of the numerous forms of approximate rhyme, moreover, are so various as to make this device very hard to control. The English reader simply can't *trust* Brodsky's practice, whatever his artistic motives may have been. I remain puzzled by the degree to which a man of Brodsky's erudition and curiosity apparently closed his mind to some obvious lessons of comparative linguistics. The legendary untranslatability of Pushkin, for instance, was a commonplace well before Brodsky's time.

7.

Tributes on the deaths of our poets tend, if they appear at all, to be motivated by personal affection rather than artistic gratitude; Eliot's death, I think, inspired no particular feelings of loss. He was still a target for respect but had not for a long while been a source of energy. Almost all poets will have absorbed, early on, his contribution to the relocation of English poetry at the beginning of the century, a contribution completed mainly within its second decade. It should be said that that relocation has been widely and continuously rejected here ever since; and that those of us who accepted it had grown used to feeling dismay or embarrassment in the face of much of Eliot's subsequent activity, which could be read as a sustained if implicit disavowal and concreting-over of his own talent.

I can't comment on the needs of Russian poetry at the time Brodsky formed his attachment to Eliot's work. It's easy to see the appeal of virtually anything external to Russia; in the 1980s in Romania and the German Democratic Republic I witnessed shows of Anglophilia which seemed bizarre in themselves but quite understandable.

8.

The state of English in the seventeenth century as a literary language—its reach, its power of rhythm, vocabulary and figuration and its ability to engage with a time of cultural turbulence—is the envy of English-speaking poets today, in a time of weakened consonants, liquescent constructions, a vocabulary of desiccated dead metaphors. The old language can't be revived except by pastiche. It's a ruinous temple which moderns can visit and where they can engage in whatever reveries seem right. Brodsky did this; it probably strengthened his technical confidence.

9.

Auden in the 1930s had an astonishing power of commanding attention and producing an effect previously, I think, unknown, although the contributory influences were always apparent. He made his text open on to a world which would appear as something other than the consensus-world implicit in realism or pastoral, though not fantastic. This world was one of imperatives far stronger than those of the consensus-world: an effect he created by various gestures of domination—sometimes outright hectoring, sometimes closure-devices such as sudden evaluations-by-adjective, which, when applied to vague or ominous material, could galvanize and intimidate the reader. Such a poetic had the power to penetrate the language-barrier, and it clearly did so for Brodsky. Auden's approach at that time was usually employed didactically, but its effect extended beyond the thematic to the business of his writing in general: he gave the impression of being licensed to write on whatever subject and in whatever manner he chose—an arrogation supported by his intellectual and technical virtuosity. All this will have had an appeal for Brodsky, working in the context of an official, historically determined public language.

That said, I'm less happy about Auden as a direct influence on Brodsky's writing (or on anybody's). Auden's early work was so singular that any attempt to imitate it could only achieve caricature; and while it would be wrong to suggest that the nature of that work was wholly determined by his homosexuality and his class background and education I've no doubt that those factors—unavailable to anybody who didn't share them—made a contribution to the sharply focused tone and the tension which characterized his literary identity: he wrote out of that milieu and addressed it in return. After he moved to America, to cruise a more generalized civilization, the tension gradually subsided and the focus diffused: much of his later work is discursive, conversational, honorific or occasional, with the earlier tone surviving as a habitually mannered surface. This was a style more available for adoption by others, and I presume it gave Brodsky a hint for the pace and texture of longer pieces.

10.

I've read only the Auden essays. 'To Please a Shadow' is, of course, mainly a piece of autobiography. It characterizes Auden well, without being exhaustive. The explication of 'September 1, 1939' is compelling as a set of flights around the text; I think its slow dramatization of the poem's progression makes it seem more laboured and packed than it is, or than I imagine Auden wanted it to appear.

11.

Tangentially to this question, I find it quite easy to conceive of a more compact, less paradoxical Brodsky by considering him straightforwardly as a Jewish, rather than a Russian writer—a very late emigré. If we imagine a man of Brodsky's talents and temperament whose grandparents had left Russia for, say, Chicago before the First World War, then the late 1970s might still have found him taking up his post at Ann Arbor, with a Ph.D and a couple of award-winning Jewish-American novels to his credit, maybe stemming from the later work of Saul Bellow, or that of Philip

Roth. He probably wouldn't have needed to be a poet, having, of course, been brought up with an American, and hence less exalted view of that art.

12.

It was good, when he first arrived, to see somebody with such commitment and enthusiasm passing through a jaded scene. He didn't make me think about my own poetry. When I first heard of him I was approaching fifty and the main lines of my work had been laid down long before. And my abiding preoccupation with space, silence and nondescript materials meant that his concerns and mine hardly overlapped at all.

13.

When I first met Brodsky he was still in his thirties; he'd been ill, and was already visibly worn by stress, cigarettes and excitement. I instantly formed the opinion that he was engaged in a gambling match of some kind with his own death, for some reason I couldn't fathom—arrogance, maybe, or simple resentment at being mortal. Later meetings didn't suggest that he was winning. The news of his death reached me at a time when almost every day was removing a friend or acquaintance and surprised me only by coming so soon. I'd expected him, I suppose, to let good fortune stabilize him and allow him to save more of his life. I can't say I was moved to many thoughts about what might have been lost by way of unwritten works, but that was largely attributable to my being out of touch.

14.

I have the impression that Brodsky was always regarded as genuine, and a writer of stature by the many British poets who knew him as a character, having run across him on the circuits; but on reflection I realize that not one of them has ever sought to discuss his work. He's not alone in this. I don't know about critics: outside my circle of acquaintance.

COAT HANGER

It's unusual in English poetry nowadays to find a writer of Peter Robinson's sophistication occupying himself with what appears, at least, to be autobiography. Poets who have taken the trouble, as Robinson certainly has, to study language and apprentice themselves to its workings rather than use it as poster-paint tend to sink themselves beneath verbal surfaces and exercise a phobic avoidance of the dangers of personal pronouns and what they may lead to. It has in any case become customary to regard the authorial "I" warily as an ironic characterization or a metaphor, and just about controllable. But "you" and especially "we" are treated as chutes into a void where characters in a poem can be subjected to misrepresentation, manipulation or lies, destabilizing the poem into harangue or the author's self-delusion.

Those pronouns undoubtedly harbour the properties of potential rogue terms, capable of swelling or shrinking or dying in their seats, distorting the texture of a poem. But to regard them as under strict compulsion to do these things is something of a libel, and it's a libel to which Robinson declines to subscribe. He appears to treat the "I" "you" and "we" in as lapidary a fashion as the carefully layered words of his observations of scenery, weather and situations. Treating the pronouns in this way means they have to be given the stability and respect accorded to things; and a reader is steered away from over-dramatic reactions by this fastidiousness of the author. He doesn't psychologize much: and where he does venture into analysis of motives or emotions it's only by way of the briefest of excursions, securely supported by the structure of the poem.

It follows that although it would be possible to conjure the ghost of a biography from this work, it is clear that even from the chronological ordering of this selection, such things as narrative, development, the road to death under the mandate of the biographical imperative, do not constitute the reason for the work's existence. The language is lucid but the sketches are left unframed; the life-images are held separate and inhibited from converging to form a story with a point. If we engage for a moment in a fiction and push the summary outline of Robinson's life away into another time—any time—and another set of places—any set of places—we can see how transferable its main terms are. A somewhat peripatetic scholar and teacher with links to several academies and good reasons for living part of each year in three countries. A pair of important relationships, one of them troubled; the witnessing of an enduringly memorable crime; a single potentially catastrophic illness; a compact set of allegiances to people and places. Not dull by any means: but a life-pattern that might have been issued to at least a whole sub-class of good poets in a variety of epochs and cultures. Thus the life-events don't provide the driving force of the poems; rather they make up the terrain, a varied surface across which the poet travels, living his life but always exercising a strong disposition to make poems from somewhere close to everyday events. It's as if he carries a listening device, alert for the moments when the tectonic plates of mental experience slide quietly one beneath another to create paradoxes and complexities that call for poems to be made. These are not the ordinary urgencies of autobiography, but they are the urgencies of new creations.

I stress the evident and sustained closeness of the "I" of the poems to the empirical Peter Robinson in order to go further into the question of the position he has quietly but with full knowledge taken up on the English poetry scene, widening and strengthening his territory with each new publication, and apparently unperturbed by the absence of a share in what little vulgar success there is to be had on that scene. From the earliest poems of his we're allowed to see he appears to have had a clear idea of the terms on which he would proceed: how much of the surrounding poetical idiom he would make use of; how much of the endlessly-moving sense of tradition that accompanies and feeds or constricts all of us. His approach to the literary canon was pragmatic. He's never peddled a petulant nostalgia. Neither has he ever become seriously entangled in the paradoxical world of the often brilliant dogmatisms of theory-driven poetics; the paradox there consisting in the way exquisitely-devised concerns with arcane aesthetics are first of all moralised, then promoted as public and social issues, often in an atmosphere of crude political bluster and inter-personal venom and contempt, leading sometimes to violence.

Robinson shows himself open, as a reader, to such work and accepts or rejects it according to its merits, while clearly finding it of little relevance to his own practice. From the formalist end of the field his work may, wrongly, appear to be of a piece with what has come to be called the Official Verse Culture. This is a manner, widely practised and published over several recent decades, in which the poems, hung from their titles, propose their occasions, anecdotes, locations or general topics in a disguised version of the way a lecturer will open a subject. There can be a wide range of personal tones in this poetry, from lyricism to near-bombast, but always the telltale defining signs are present. The work's mode of operation is to display, explain and, however subtly, to judge what it addresses itself to. The mode has the characteristics of an essay, even a paraphrase. "Life" is written up, elevated a little way, into "art" in a way that in the most popular instances gives a reader a sense of value received in return for the labour of reading. There will be decoration, a packaging of figures from what Stuart Mills called "the bottomless school satchels of the metaphor-mongers"; but the Official Verse Culture depends mostly on an easy conversational style that has absorbed the relaxations, though not the excitements and constraints, of modernism. It is quite difficult to write really badly in this idiom, and it's much used, prophylactically or curatively, in Creative Writing courses.

It's easy to see how, swimming quietly along in this shoal of fish, Robinson can (as his publishing history suggests) be mistaken for part of it or even overlooked; for his work, though, in John Ashbery's words, "curiously strong", doesn't have eye-catching idiosyncrasies and is short of convenient grab-handles. He doesn't do grotesques or caricatures; he's witty enough but not particularly comic; there's no extra-poetic tag of theme or material that it's worth anybody's while to hang on him; the biographical elements are, as I've said, put to poetic rather than dramatic use. And the essayistic qualities of the style have obviously had no appeal for him. It's such features as the smoothly articulated densities of observations and mental events and the careful placing of the figure representing the empirical Peter Robinson that confirm his singularity.

I'm tempted to use pictorial similes to describe his poems. Though he's not photographic or viewy, a few visual hints will produce the limited mise-en-scène a movie director might provide, particularly in urban or interior settings, for his actors—for these poems do mostly contain people. Often the well-placed "I" is to be sensed as a shadowy presence, its back to the camera and off to one side and on watch. That's a general effect. But close attention to the visual hints will show a poet intimately involved with the physical world and its evidences. Almost at random: "a full moon / blurred above neon, pantographs, sea…", "a wall's late-modern, matt-white…", "The cypresses disordered / by stiff gusts, bedraggled strands / flurried at her face beside me", "Uncurtained, jammed sash windows / let on to Sandtex beyond the front door", "Trolley-bus cables divide that deep blue, all but black—", "the scratches in a wooden step from its entry well…", "Strings of bulbs between each frontage, / white, with a fainter halo in the air…", "ploughed piles of exhausted black snow…", and the whole first section of 'There Again'.

Robinson is a master of the absorbed metaphor, the device that, grammatically, lies hidden, absorbing the qualities of, say, a mood into itself and dispensing them informally back into the poem without a click of cleverness or a hint of the bottomless school satchel. It's a device that can be profuse, plethoric and productive of internal collisions: Robinson's choice is to use it sparingly and in such a way as to make a poem at once more physical and more lucid. A similar thing could be said about his use of adjectives, potential traps often abjured by those excellent teachers, the post-Poundians and Objectivists: "Adjectives drain nouns", said Basil Bunting. But in "dark carp swam beneath the surface / of their spacious liquid…" there's no doubt that the quickly dealt adjectives earn their right to be there.

It will be apparent that I'm disinclined to recommend a simple chronological reading of these poems of twenty-five years, or any attempt to trace lines of development, that venerable critical vice that lazily projects on to an artist's work the quasi-romantic model of a quest composed of challenges, agonies, successes, crises and failures. Robinson's work simply blocks that option. Individual poems have individual lives, individual musical qualities. In the absence of repetitious, empty or vacuously occasional pieces each work can be seen as something added to the world rather than a mere notebook page of commentary upon it.

Inevitably, though, there are changes in practice. The terms of engagement, already clear in the earliest work still in print, are at that stage held almost defensively close in the interests of definition and the avoidance of flooding by extraneous elements: the "drawing" can be austere, even stiff, with third-person constructions keeping characters at a distance. This position, since it was, I take it, pragmatic rather than programmatic, was to be neither repudiated nor vacated: but it might have been hard to see it as predictive of the richness, variety, suppleness and cultural inclusiveness of later work. I think of the sly, unfashionable rhymes that come to the attention only after they've already been at their work for a few stanzas; and the moments of easy-going Eliot pastiche in 'Via Sauro Variations', where Eliot is simply recruited and used, with no ironic purpose that I can detect. Then there's the extraordinarily complex 'Coat Hanger', a veritable aquarium of shifting images and potential associations, circling away into long regressions, and hung from its ending in an understated tour de force, an audacious play on a single word in William Carlos Williams's 'The Red Wheelbarrow' and thus, in turn, on the infinity of ideas available to readers of that poem. And back to the beginning of 'Coat Hanger' to see how what we thought was the poem has been altered by the revelation at its conclusion. This is far more than a domestic vignette.

A Checklist of Roy Fisher's Occasional Prose

Derek Slade

Mermaid, 18:1, Birmingham, October 1951, pp. 1-2. Editorial.

Tlaloc, 13, n.d. (*c.* 1966), Leeds, unpaginated. Review of *Twenty Words: Twenty Days* by Gael Turnbull.

'Style and Narrative Viewpoint in the Later Novels of Norman Mailer', MA thesis, University of Birmingham, 1970.

The Cut Pages, London: Fulcrum Press 1971, pp. 6-7. 'Note'.

Language and Style, 6:2, 1973. 'The Mind of Marion Faye: Stylistic Aspects of Norman Mailer's *The Deer Park*'.

Vole, 4, 1977, ed. Richard Boston, pp. 38-39. 'Brum Born'.

Journal of American Studies, 12:2, August 1978, pp. 254-56. Review of *An Autobiographical Novel* by Kenneth Rexroth.

Poetry Book Society Bulletin, 99, Christmas 1978, unpaginated. 'Roy Fisher writes…' (brief commentary on *The Thing about Joe Sullivan*).

Journal of American Studies, 14:2, August 1980, pp. 325-26. Review of *Robert Creeley's Poetry: A Critical Introduction* by Cynthia Dubin Edelberg.

Powys Review, 11, Lampeter, Dyfed, 1982-83, pp. 86-87. Review of *Englishman's Road* by Jeremy Hooker.

Stand, 25:1, Newcastle upon Tyne, Winter 1983-84, pp. 51-53. Review of *Dada and After* by Alan Young.

The Beau, 3, Dublin, 1983-84, pp. 6-10. Three extracts from *Talks for Words*.

1985 Prizewinners, Poetry Society, London, 1985. Includes an account by RF of his experience of judging (with Tom Paulin and Carol Rumens) the 1985 Poetry Competition.

A Birmingham Dialogue, Birmingham: Protean Pubs, 1986. By Paul Lester and Roy Fisher. This pamphlet contains 'The Poetry of Roy Fisher' (pp.5-20), an undergraduate dissertation by Paul Lester written in 1974, and 'Reply to Paul Lester by Roy Fisher' (pp. 21-29) written in 1985.

The Cut Pages (2nd ed.), London: Oasis Books/Shearsman Books, 1986. Prefatory note (unpaginated).

A Furnace, Oxford: Oxford University Press, 1986, pp. vii-viii. 'Preface'.

Numbers, 2, Cambridge, Spring 1987, pp. 24-28. 'Handsworth Compulsions'.

Beat Dreams and Plymouth Sounds: An Anthology, ed. Alexis Lykiard. Devon, Plymouth Arts Centre, 1987, unpaginated. 'Note on "Variations"'.

The Independent (no. 520), Friday, 10 June 1988. 'The Power of Speech'.

The Jazz Rag, 10 September 1989, p.21. Review of *Beat Goes Poetry*, a recording of the Cellar Jazz Quintet with readings by Kenneth Rexroth and Lawrence Ferlinghetti.

Contemporary Authors (Autobiography Series), 10, Detroit, New York, Fort Lauderdale, London: Gale Research Inc., 1989, pp. 79-100.

Spleen (2nd ed.,) by Nicholas Moore. London, Menard Press, 1990, pp. 8-10. 'Foreword'. An on-line version is available at http://www.ubu.com/ubu/pdf/moore_spleen.pdf.

High on the Walls: A Morden Tower Anthology, ed. Gordon Brown. Newcastle upon Tyne: Morden Tower/Bloodaxe Books, 1990, p. 57. Note on reading at the Morden Tower.

Poets on Writing: Britain, 1970-1991, ed. Denise Riley. London: Macmillan, 1992, pp. 272-75. Chapter 35, 'Poet on Writing'.

The Jazz Anthology, ed. Miles Kington. London: Harper and Collins, 1992, pp. 29-32, 48-49, 105-09, 210-211. Contains five sections from 'Remembrance of Gigs Past'. Date of original broadcasts wrongly given as 1970; correct year 1988.

What Poets Eat, ed. Judi Benson. London: Foolscap, 1994, p. 23. 'The Heavy Spinach Soup' (recipe).

Secret Files, collection of poems by Eleanor Cooke. London: Jonathan Cape, 1974. Brief comment by RF on back jacket:

> Secret Files *initially has, of necessity, something of a biblical* mise-en-scène. *For all that, it's a peculiarly English grotesque of the Kilpeck sort, carried out with an imaginative freedom that goes beyond the contemporary mischief of its main premise ... Eleanor Cooke is in confident and sometimes hilarious free flight.*

Sons of Ezra: British Poets and Ezra Pound, ed. Michael Alexander and James McGonical. Amsterdam: Rodopi, 1995, pp. 41-42.

Contemporary Poets (6th edn.), ed. Thomas Riggs, Detroit: St James Press, 1996, p. 345. Commentary on his procedure as a poet.

The Rialto, 35, Autumn 1996, Norwich, pp. 30-32. 'Roy Fisher Reviews Roy Fisher' (a self-review by RF of *The Dow Low Drop*). This was also published in the Bloodaxe 1997 catalogue (pp.34-35).

Stand, 38:2, Newcastle upon Tyne, Spring 1997, pp. 44-46. Review of *Collected Poems and Translations* by A. C. Jacobs.

The London, poem by David Rees (West House Books and Gratton Street Irregulars, 1997). Brief comment on back cover:

> *As London festers on, easier now to marvel at than visit, the intelligent poet picks on patches to squeeze, and to pinch with shocked and satisfied rhymes; scars, sacs, rust, light, old idea-stains. There's one been going about and does a certain operation.*

Good to see parts of that city pinned in, with no chances for evasion. These brick-sized graffiti.

Poets on Poets, ed. Nick Rennison and Michael Schmidt. Manchester: Carcanet Press, 1997, pp. 60-62. Brief essay on the work of Thomas Campion, p. 60, and a selection by RF of Campion's poetry, pp. 61-62.

When Suzy Was, Kelvin Corcoran. Kentisbeare, Devon: Shearsman Books, 1999. Comment on back cover:

> *There is a clear sad music playing right through this book of answers, steady and unmistakable. Against it, the urges of friendship, love and harsh judgements move sharp and bright with their own turbulences and poignancies, in the air of an unstoppered past. If Corcoran takes himself into a timeless Greece it's not with the intention of fooling himself: he's an honest visitor to the oracle.*

Interviews Through Time, and Selected Prose, ed. Tony Frazer. Kentisbeare, Devon: Shearsman Books, 2000. The prose pieces collected in this book are the autobiographical essay published in *Contemporary Authors*, five of the *Talks for Words* (number four is excluded) and the self-review published in *The Rialto*.

News for the Ear: A Homage to Roy Fisher, ed. Peter Robinson and Robert Sheppard, Exeter, Stride Publications, 2000. 'Licence my Roving Hands' (a revised version of 'Remembrance of Gigs Past') pp. 18-44.

The Star You Steer By: Basil Bunting and British Modernism, ed. James McGonical and Richard Price. Amsterdam/Atlanta GA: Rodopi, 2001. 'Debt to Mr Bunting', pp. 11-16.

Poet's Poems 6, series edited by Stuart Mills. Derbyshire: Aggie Weston's Editions, 2001. Unpaginated. RF provides a brief postscript on his choice of poems:*

> *I suppose what they have in common is that I've never taught, or been taught, any of them. So they're not too polluted.*
>
> ** The poems are: Thomas Campion, 'Rose-Cheeked Laura', Anonymous, 'Clerk Saunders', William Blake, 'The Mental Traveller', Ben Jonson, 'A Fit of Rime against Rime', Adrian Mitchell, 'The Eggs O'God', Thomas Wyatt, 'They fle from me...', Anonymous, 'The Bailey Beareth the Bell Away', and Basil Bunting, conclusion to 'Chomei at Toyama'.*

Jacket 22, May 2003. 'Prose memoir' [of Richard Caddel]. Available at http://jacketmagazine.com/22/caddel.html.

Selected Poems by Jeff Nuttall. Cambridge: Salt Publications, 2004. Introduction, p. xvii.

Islands by Stuart Montgomery. Exbourne: Etruscan Books, 2005. Blurb comment by RF:

> *Stuart Montgomery's singularity is that there seems to have been an uncannily clear and intense perception, formed early and in part practiced even before the setting-*

up of Fulcrum Press. This conviction, arrived at then with no need for polemic, has survived the passage of decades without signs of any impulse to modify or trim. The later verse moves at the same quiet vigilant pace as the earlier and the voice is unaltered. This is an unusually assured, aware and compact work.

There are Words: Collected Poems, Gael Turnbull. Exeter: Shearsman Books, 2006. Back cover contains a tribute to Gael Turnbull by RF.

Starting at Zero, ed. Nicholas Johnson. Exbourne: Etruscan Books, 2007. Contains 'At A Tangent', a brief account of RF's responses to the Black Mountain poets.

The Salt Companion to Peter Robinson, ed. Adam Piette and Katy Price. Cambridge: Salt Publications, 2007. Preface, pp. 21-25.

Down to Earth, John Wilkinson. Cambridge: Salt Publications, 2008. Commendatory sentence by RF. The sentence is taken from the interview with John Kerrigan published in *News for the Ear: A Homage to Roy Fisher* and also available on-line as part of *Jacket* magazine:

John Wilkinson's a powerful and intent poet whose language is densely charged with energy-traces: it's rich with verbs, the sense of happenings, deeds, potentialities, necessities, results.

The Powys Journal, Vol. 18, 2008. 'On JCP's Letters (with two letters from JCP to Fisher)', pp. 30-37. RF discusses his correspondence with John Cowper Powys.

Uplift: A Samizdat for Lee Harwood from his Friends, ed. Patricia Hope Scanlan. Hove: Artery Editions, 2008. 'My Trip to Brighton', p. 10.

An Unofficial Roy Fisher, ed. Peter Robinson. Exeter: Shearsman Books, 2010. 'Death by Adjectives', pp. 80-83.

David Prentice: 'The Green Fuse' published by The John Davies Gallery, Moreton-in-Marsh, Gloucestershire, 2010. This catalogue of an exhibition of paintings by David Prentice contains an appreciation by RF, pp. 5-9.

Cusp: Recollections of Poetry in Transition, ed. Geraldine Monk. Bristol: Shearsman Books, 2012. 'Meanwhile', pp. 32-34.

Locklines, Canal & River Trust and Chrysalis Art, no date given but c. 2012/2013. No pagination. Brief statement by RF on being commissioned to write a poem for the Locklines project:

In addition to letting me think again about the canals among which I grew up, this commission suited my habitual verbal stinginess. Often when I've collaborated with artists and designers I've noticed that my texts, initially at least, seemed brief; but here the compulsory limitation to a small number of actual characters made me feel at home.

See also the following item.

Locklines—Lockgates Blog. 'Down the Cut' (dated 15 September 2012). Two paragraphs by RF on his childhood experience of canals. Available at: http://www.locklines.org.uk/lockgates-blog.html.

Untitled prose paragraph on Christopher Middleton in *Tributes to Christopher Middleton, The Bow Wow Shop* (Michael Glover's website). Available at: http://www.bowwowshop.org.uk/page10.htm.

I owe CM a debt of understanding. At a time when the Sunday broadsheets still carried reviews of new poetry there appeared a review of his book Torse #3. *The piece was by its own standards civilised: but it was patronising, ignorant, insular and weary. I had at that time virtually no contacts and no prospect of getting a book published; but I was working tentatively in a distant corner of the same territory, and the review showed me in an instant how the cards were stacked. It freed me from setting any store by opinions that might come from such a quarter.*

Lightning Source UK Ltd.
Milton Keynes UK
UKOW03f2226190914

238904UK00001B/31/P